101 WAYS TO BECOME A WORLD CHAMPION

RICHARD HAPPER

Published by Collins
An imprint of HarperCollins Publishers
Westerhill Road
Bishopbriggs
Glasgow G64 2QT
collins.reference@harpercollins.co.uk
www.harpercollins.co.uk

First edition 2016

© HarperCollins Publishers 2016
Text written by Richard Happer 2016
Design by Gavin James 2016

A catalogue record for this book is available from the British Library

ISBN 978-0-00-819182-5

10 9 8 7 6 5 4 3 2 1

Printed in China by RR Donnelley APS Co. Ltd

Front cover and title page image: © REX Shutterstock; front flap
cover image: © Jeff Morgan 05 / Alamy; back flap cover image:
© Mark Gledhill; front inside cover image: © Nick Turner / Alamy;
back inside cover image: © Photocase Addicts GmbH / Alamy;
cover and title font: © Olly Molly / Shutterstock

MIX
Paper from
responsible sources
FSC
www.fsc.org   **FSC™ C007454**

FSC™ is a non-profit international organisation established to promote the
responsible management of the world's forests. Products carrying the FSC
label are independently certified to assure consumers that they come from
forests that are managed to meet the social, economic and ecological needs
of present and future generations, and other controlled sources.

Find out more about HarperCollins and the environment at
www.harpercollins.co.uk/green

CONTENTS

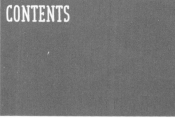

14 | outhouse racing
(Nevada, U.S.)

15 | stinging nettle eating
(Dorset, England)

16 | mobile phone throwing
(Finland)

17 | tree climbing
(U.S.)

18 | extreme ironing
(England, Germany)

19 | rock, paper, scissors
(U.S., Canada)

20 | pooh sticks
(Oxfordshire, England)

21 | pig squealing
(France)

22 | muggle quidditch
(U.S.)

23 | winter swimming
(Finland, Russia)

24 | bog snorkelling
(Wales)

25 | pillow fighting
(California, U.S.)

26 | shin kicking
(Gloucestershire, England)

27 | latte art
(worldwide)

28 | rock stacking
(Texas, U.S.)

29 | air guitar
(Finland)

30 | paper plane throwing
(Austria)

31 | sheep shearing
(New Zealand)

32 | shoe repairing
(U.S.)

33 | coal carrying
(Yorkshire, England)

34 | ugliest dog
(California, U.S.)

35 | fly-casting
(Norway, Estonia)

36 | lifesaving
(worldwide)

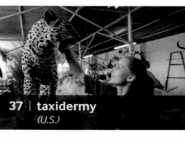

37 | taxidermy
(U.S.)

38 | paragliding accuracy
(worldwide)

39 | mini golf
(Finland, Sweden, Germany)

40 | goanna pulling
(Australia)

41 | drone racing
(Hawaii, U.S.)

42 | cheese rolling
(Gloucestershire, England)

43 | lumberjacking
(Wisconsin, U.S.)

44 | tin bathtub racing
(Isle of Man)

45 | cherry-pit spitting
(U.S., Switzerland)

46 | combat juggling
(worldwide)

47 | toe wrestling
(Derbyshire, England)

48 | ferret-legging
(Yorkshire, England)

49 | sled dog racing
(Alaska, U.S.)

50 | sand sculpting
(Canada)

51 | public speaking
(U.S.)

52 | peashooting
(Cambridgeshire, England)

53 | dog dancing
(worldwide)

54 | freestyle soccer
(worldwide)

55 | octopush
(worldwide)

56 | marbles
(West Sussex, England)

57 | cake decorating
(Italy)

58 | handwriting
(New York, U.S.)

59 | **kaninhop**
(Sweden)

60 | **boardgaming**
(Pennsylvania, U.S.)

61 | **disc golf**
(U.S., Canada)

62 | **conkers**
(Northamptonshire, England)

63 | **gurning**
(Cumbria, England)

64 | **lawnmower racing**
(West Sussex, England)

65 | **chessboxing**
(worldwide)

66 | **sport stacking**
(worldwide)

67 | **yo-yo**
(worldwide)

68 | **window cleaning**
(Florida, U.S.)

69 | **grits rolling**
(South Carolina, U.S.)

70 | **mountain unicycling**
(Canada)

71 | **wood chopping**
(Australia)

72 | **karaoke**
(worldwide)

73 | **wine tasting**
(France)

74 | shovel racing
(New Mexico, U.S.)

75 | cockroach racing
(Australia)

76 | deer calling
(Europe-wide)

77 | tent pitching
(London, England)

78 | extreme pogo
(U.S.)

79 | chainsaw carving
(Wisconsin, U.S.)

80 | tree felling
(Switzerland)

81 | bagpiping
(Scotland)

82 | street luge
(worldwide)

83 | dry riverbed racing
(Australia)

84 | powersliding
(Norway)

85 | cycle polo
(worldwide)

86 | egg throwing
(Lincolnshire, England)

87 | quizzing
(worldwide)

88 | tiddlywinks
(England, U.S.)

INTRODUCTION

Are your picnics often spoiled because bees seem to find you irresistible? Well, far from this being an annoying thing that you just have to put up with, it could be the talent that makes you a world champion. You see, "bee wearing," where you have to attract as many of the stinging, striped insects onto your body as possible, is very much a competitive thing.

Do you own a rabbit? It loves hopping doesn't it? Well, maybe it's talented enough to win the world championship in bunny jumping, otherwise known as kaninhop! Are you awesome at air guitar? If you can recreate the solo of *Stairway to Heaven* without actually playing an instrument, then get yourself up on stage for the Air Guitar World Championships. Have you ever had a pillow fight? Decorated a cake? Played a boardgame? Entered a pub quiz? Made a speech? Ironed a shirt? Then international glory and fame could await you...

It turns out there are lots of weird and wonderful sports and activities of which you can become a world champion. Many of these don't require any particular skill – a schoolgirl has as much chance of becoming a world pooh sticks champion as a professional soccer player. And being an elite athlete might actually count against you when it comes to running the Beer Mile – a highly developed alcohol tolerance is what you need for that one. This is great news for those of us who have no ability at the more traditional forms of sports, such as soccer, but might just be crazy and determined enough to excel at swamp soccer, where you basically play the game in a bog. Or indeed bog snorkelling, which you could also have a go at while you're in that quagmire.

In this book, we give you a taste of 101 such events, explaining their rules and origin. We also offer some top tips from previous world champions and a guide to the techniques you'll need to master if you want to become one yourself. So, if you can't throw a discus but can skip a mean stone, dive into these pages and see if you can make a splash in a weird sport.

Then, on some future day, when you are standing on that podium with the crowd chanting your name, a gold medal around your neck and your parents shedding proud tears, you can look back on this book as the nudge you needed down your path to everlasting glory.

Good luck. Now go become a world champion.

You can't deny that there's a real buzz around these champions.

Who brought the jam sandwiches?

Do you have what it takes to have 100,000 stinging insects crawling, buzzing and swarming over your bare skin? Could you stand still for a full hour while they do so, fighting the natural human urge to scratch, run away or dive into the nearest lake in panic? Then perhaps you have what it takes to be a world champion bee wearer.

How it started

For as long as humans have kept bees in hives, beekeepers have calmly allowed bees to rest on their bodies to show their understanding and tolerance of the insects.

In the 1830s, Petro Prokopovych, a Ukrainian beekeeper, turned this apian aptitude into a competitive endeavor. It was he who first allowed measurable quantities of bees to gather on his face. The practice became known as "bee bearding." Throughout the nineteenth century the skill was a regular feature at American carnivals where it was exhibited as one of the freak shows. It is still demonstrated at agricultural shows around the world today, as well as in record-breaking attempts and competitions.

As competitors pushed themselves to attract ever-greater numbers of bees, the sport moved beyond the basic "beard" and most advanced competitors now attract bees to their entire face, torso, back and arms. To those in the game, however, it is still known as "bee bearding."

How to bee a winner

The first thing to know is that the bees you attract to your body aren't counted, but weighed. This is for two reasons: firstly, bees differ in size from country to country, and secondly, it is very, very hard to count up to 100,000 bees when they are swarming around all over the place. So competitors stand on a set of scales and their progress in the competition can be calculated according to their increase in weight.

Beekeepers bring several hives of bees to the outdoor venue. Before the event the bees should be fed with a can of sugar syrup. Well-fed bees are less likely to sting, so it's a good idea to keep them fat and happy. The bees then have to be encouraged to leave their hives and alight on you. This is done by placing a queen bee in a small cage and strapping this under your chin. The bees are attracted to the queen's pheromones and duly start to swarm.

Competitive bee bearders usually also don underwear, goggles, nose and ear plugs, and sometimes, a back brace.

When you've won the title, unstrap the queen in her cage and put her back in the hive. The bees should follow her, but you can encourage them to depart by jumping up and down a little. Any stragglers can be removed with a soft brush.

The world beater

The Guinness Book of Records has a category for "most pounds of bees worn on the body." On 13 May 2014, Ruan Liangming, a Chinese beekeeper from Fengxin county of Jiangxi province broke the world record by covering himself with 26.8 kg (59 lb) of bees. His robe of swarming insects contained over 100,000 bees and he lasted more than fifty-three minutes.

So, the big question – do bee wearers get stung? The answer is yes, usually dozens of times. You just have to remain calm, don't panic and focus on the glory of becoming a world champion...

Climb aboard, my dear

Race over the rocks and across the sand, wade through the pond, clear several fences, splash through the brook and complete the gruelling course in one minute to beat the rest of the pack and be crowned champion. One final thing – you have to do the whole event carrying your wife on your back.

How it started

Wife carrying is a Finnish creation – the local term for the sport is *eukonkanto* – and it was first developed in Sonkajärvi, a wooded, rural part of eastern Finland speckled with hundreds of lakes.

The race was inspired by the actions of a nineteenth-century bandit leader, Herkko Rosvo-Ronkainen, who lived deep in the forests of Finland. Herkko and his gang of brigands survived by sneaking out of the forest and raiding local villages. Far from being a Robin Hood type, he stole from those who were well-off and kept the booty for himself. Depending on their appetites, the bandits would pinch bags of food or any passing women who took their fancy. Their over-the-shoulder getaway tactic was the same for both types of plunder.

A less lascivious version of the tale holds that Rosvo-Ronkainen trained his followers to be stronger and faster in their nefarious activities by carrying heavy sacks on their backs. This became a rural endurance sport, which eventually turned into the celebratory event we see today.

Whatever the legend, the modern wife-carrying world championships were inaugurated in Sonkajärvi in 1992.

Know the rules

The objective is for the male to carry the female around an obstacle course in the fastest time. Two couples run at a time, creating multiple mini-races that add to the excitement of the overall best-time-wins event. Your prize, should you triumph, as well as ultimate glory, is your wife's weight in beer.

This isn't just a young man-and-wife's game – there is a senior championship for competitors aged 40 and over. There are also special awards for the most entertaining couple, the best costume, and the strongest carrier.

The minimum weight of the wife to be carried is 49 kg (108 lb). If she weighs less than that, she must wear a rucksack containing additional weight to bring the total load to be carried up to 49 kg.

The championship rules are very clear about the provenance of the wife to be toted around the course: "the wife to be carried may be your own, your neighbor's or you may have found her farther afield; she must, however, be over 17 years of age."

Perhaps the most important rule is this one: "All participants must enjoy themselves."

Tips on technique

A solid carrying style is crucial. Dropping your wife will lose you vital seconds, as well as potentially causing her some discomfort. The style you choose depends on several factors,

This wasn't what she had in mind when you said you'd give her a lift to the store.

17

including the relative sizes of the couple and personal athletic preference. Petite wives may be best carried piggyback. A good general style is the fireman's carry over the shoulder. The most popular choice is the "Estonian method" where the wife hangs upside-down with her legs around the husband's shoulders, holding onto his waist. It is the Fosbury Flop of wife carrying and legend has it that this was perfected by Estonian husbands who used it to carry their darlings home over rugged terrain.

Where and when to make your challenge

The original blue riband event is held every July in Sonkajärvi. If you can't make it to eastern Finland, you can also enter wife-carrying championships in Maine, Wisconsin and Michigan in the U.S., Kerala in India, Hong Kong, Estonia, the UK and Australia. The Australian event has levelled the gender playing field with the complementary inclusion of a husband-dragging contest.

Taisto Miettinen from Finland, five-time wife-carrying world champion and record holder (with his partner Kristiina Haapanen), recommends training for the event wearing ski boots.

WHERE ARIZONA, U.S. | **EQUIPMENT** SADDLE, REINS, OSTRICH
DANGERS UNPREDICTABLE STEED, LIONS

Bird-brained

This might seem like a sport thought up by some zany South African guys who'd had a few too many Castle Lagers, but ostrich racing is actually over two millennia old. Archaeologists investigating an ancient tomb unearthed a statue of the Egyptian queen Arsinoe II (born in 316 BC) riding an ostrich.

It may be ancient, but it sure isn't easy. With a top speed of 70 km/h (43 mph), the ostrich is the world's fastest two-legged animal. It stands up to 2.74 m (9 ft) in height, weighs up to 154 kg (340 lb) and offers a very bumpy ride – each stride can be 5 m (16 ft) long. You ride an ostrich as you would a horse, with a saddle, reins and a bit, but an ostrich is much more unpredictable than your average dobbin. Your bird may suddenly decide to stop entirely for no good reason, go backwards, sideways or even drop flat to the ground. Be careful if you're thrown: in the wild, ostriches often defend themselves against predators with their powerful kick and have even been known to kill lions. Which all adds to the excitement of the race, of course.

Ride him, cowboy

The Chandler Ostrich Festival in Arizona has been running for twenty-eight years, and is one of the world's best giant bird-racing occasions. The racing itself is strictly for experienced riders, so if you want to learn the ropes you'd best head to South Africa, where there are several places you can get your leg up on an ostrich, including Oudtshoorn in the Karoo desert region.

Saddle up on the world's largest living bird and get ready for the ride of your life.

Did you know? The ostrich-racing scene in the Disney movie *Prince of Persia: The Sands of Time* was filmed using Moroccan horse jockeys as stuntmen.

Being fat is an absolute positive

It is the nature of sporting endeavor to try one's best in the face of adversity. But to bring that adversity on yourself – in fact, to *put* that adversity on yourself – shows a peculiar commitment to the sporting ideal. For the concept behind Sumo Suit Athletics is that you complete several track-and-field events while wearing the kit that is absolutely least suited for you to be able to do so – a heavy, cumbersome and sweat-inducing comedy-foam sumo suit.

The 11-kg (24.3-lb) suit minimizes arm and leg movements, which maximizes the comedy. And that is really the name of the game here. The real competition is in who can make a laughing stock of themselves the fastest. It's no wonder that Sumo

It's all about making a fool of yourself as fast as you can.

Suit Athletics has been embraced (albeit somewhat awkwardly) by the stag-do fraternity.

However, the World Championships are a very real competition, with five main events: 100-m sprint, long jump, high jump, shot put and the 400-m endurance race. Nor are the world records to be belly-laughed at: the 100-m record is a gut-bustingly good 14.43 seconds, set by Ed Moyse of Great Britain in 2010 at the World Championships.

Did you know? Japan is not the spiritual home of Sumo Suit Athletics: that honor falls to Battersea Park in South London, where the World Championships have been held since 2008.

5 | BABY CRAWLING

WHERE HONG KONG

AGE OF COMPETITORS 6 MONTHS – 1 YEAR AND 4 MONTHS | **RACE DISTANCE** 3 M (3.3 YD.)

Baby, you can move

Champions often take up their sport early in life. Usain Bolt was his school 100 m champ aged 12. Jessica Ennis-Hill took to the track at 10. Chris Hoy was a BMX star by the age of 7. But none of them started this early: the world baby-crawling championships are open to competitors when they reach just 6 months old.

The sport is deceptively simple: babies must crawl as fast as they can down a lane towards the finish line. Lanes are colored differently and the finish line may be decorated with flowers, ribbons or other attractions. Usually one parent sets the baby off, the other stands at the finish line, holding attractive toys, stuffed bears and pieces of fruit in a bid to have their child actually complete the race.

The sport is big in China, where "tiger mothers" push their youngsters to the limit, and in the U.S. the races are known as "diaper derbies." In 2015, Japan hosted the largest-ever baby-crawling competition, when 600 juniors wriggled and jiggled their way to the finish line. But Hong Kong hosts the father (and mother) of all events. It was founded in 1998, and to be a true world champion this is the one you need to win.

Tears of frustration, whoops of laughter, unexpected bodily fluids — no other sport on earth has so much of them all.

Young at heart

Of course, if you're reading this you are far too old to enter this event yourself. But perhaps your progeny will have the talent to succeed, and you can vicariously bask in their world-champion glory. (You certainly won't be the first parent to do so.)

Before the race, the competitors limber up. Tactics vary here. Some racers favor sucking their own toes. Others warm up their biceps and triceps by pulling mama's hair.

Motivation is a problem for some athletes. While their coaches wait at the finish line in expectation of a committed performance, a few entrants seem more interested in their neighbor's socks, the overhead lighting or, indeed, their own shadow.

A starting gun might reduce the field to tears, so the race officials get things underway by shaking a rattle. As soon as the first clack echoes around the auditorium, the coaches (parents, really) burst out cooing and ah-ing, encouraging their prostrate protégés to wobble into action.

Sometimes the pressure gets too much. Suddenly the leader stops in her tracks. A pained then a placid look passes over her face. The rest of the field is closing… her parents are yelling at her to keep racing… but the pack has caught her… they've gone past! What's happened to her? Then, a tell-tale aroma drifts through the stadium. Contestant number 7 has filled her diaper. She flumps down to have a good cry about it. Her race is over.

For the winner, victory is sweet. Well, sweets. But any fame is destined to be fleeting, for although these competitors are feisty, they are scrupulously sporting. To them, the glory of victory and the emptiness of defeat are borne in exactly the same way. With a nap.

My, what big teeth you have

All you have to do is put your chin on top of your partner's nose, extend your arms, hold the pose and you could be in with a good chance of becoming a world champ. The only trouble is that your co-competitor is a feisty, ferocious and fully toothed American alligator.

It might seem like the creation of a back-swamp fever-dream, but alligator wrestling actually has a noble history: the Seminole and Miccosukee Indians invented the sport centuries ago. The ancient practice was updated as a competitive spectacle by James Holt, a Native American whose family has wrestled the creatures for decades. ("Can I interest anyone in a game of bridge after dinner tonight?" "No, mother, I have a better idea!" is presumably how that came about…)

This is obviously not something that you can just try your hand at. Chances are you'll lose that hand. You need to head down to Florida and get some serious gator-grappling practice. This is best done with the alligator's mouth taped shut. And your own eyes very wide open. If you make the grade in training you can join the real contenders in the competition pit with the monster.

First you have to remove your gator from a deep pool and bring it onto land. Now it's time to dance with death and pull off some daring stunts. Your moves will be judged in five different categories: alligator aggressiveness, water wrangling, land wrangling, wrestler style and difficulty of stunts. As if this wasn't hard enough, you have only eight minutes to prove you are a world-class beastmaster.

If you triumph, your reward will be a cash prize and the adulation of a live audience of 2,500 people. Not to mention the reassuring knowledge that you can still play the piano.

Where tribal tradition meets extreme sport.

Did you know? American alligators can measure up to 4.6 m (15 ft) in length and weigh up to 453 kg (999 lb).

Smoothly does it

Were you a pretty good pitcher at baseball? Perhaps you were handy at fielding in cricket, but not batting or bowling? Then Easdale, a gem of an island in the windswept and wonderful Hebrides, is the place for you. This is the home of the World Stone Skimming Championships, where glory is yours if you can simply skim a stone further across the water than anyone else.

From the air, the tiny isle looks to have been almost hollowed out – it is dotted with huge, water-filled gouges. These were once thriving slate quarries, but no stones have been taken out of here since the 1950s. In fact, now the trend is to throw them back in again.

The island's geology means there is an almost limitless number of flat slate stones peppering the island, washed smooth by the sea. They are absolutely perfect for skimming, and a water-filled quarry makes the ideal venue. The World Stone Skimming Championships were founded here in 1983 and are now run by the island community as a fundraising event. The contest is open to anyone, no matter their age. There are categories for children and veterans, who compete for the "Old Tosser Walking Stick." The island's population of seventy people welcomes 350 competitors from twenty countries.

Your stone must bounce at least three times to count, and it's then all about how far across the quarry it gets before sinking. A throw of 25 m (82 ft) is respectable. A 30-m (98.4-ft) skim would probably get you on the women's podium. Supremely skilled skimmers will hit the quarry's back wall, 65 m (200 ft) away. The king of the skim is Scotland's own Dougie Isaacs, a seven-time champion.

If discovering a perfectly
smooth, flat skimming
stone on a beach makes
your heart skip, then this is
the championship for you.

27

Skipping school

As any schoolchild can tell you, the key to a good skip is spinning the stone. This gives it stability in the air, like a Frisbee. When the stone hits the water, spin keeps it angled on its trailing edge instead of somersaulting. Even if the throw isn't ideal, a decent spin rate can help correct a stone's flight before it hits the water.

Physicist Lydéric Bocquet has calculated that for a stone to skip five times it has to spin five times per second; to skip fifteen times, it has to spin almost nine times per second. According to this formula, the world record-setting throw (by Texas-born Jerdone McGhee) was spinning nearly fourteen times a second and moving at nearly 44 km/h (27 mph).

According to to Bocquet, the conditions for skipping depend on a stone's diameter (α), velocity (V), mass (M), tilt (θ), angle of attack (β), and the density of water (P_w).

$$V_{x0} > V_c = \frac{\sqrt{\dfrac{16Mg}{\pi C p_\omega \alpha^2}}}{\sqrt{1 - \dfrac{8M\tan^2\beta}{\pi \alpha^3 C p_\omega \sin\theta}}}$$

Did you know? Engineer Sir Barnes Wallis often skipped rocks with his grandchildren. During the Second World War, he used the principles of the activity to create "bouncing bombs" that destroyed German dams.

World
Worm Charming
Championships at
Willaston County
Primary School

8 | WORM CHARMING

WHERE CHESHIRE, ENGLAND | **EQUIPMENT** BUCKET, GARDEN FORK, BOOTS
QUALIFICATION STANDARDS OPEN TO ALL, INCLUDING MOLES

Entice invertebrates from the earth against the clock – if a seagull can do it, how hard can it be?

Get a wiggle on

To become a world-champion worm charmer you have to collect as many worms as possible in thirty minutes from an allocated 3 m by 3 m (9.8 ft by 9.8 ft) square of ground. This isn't done by digging, but by coaxing the creatures from the ground with vibrations. Just as seagulls and other birds do when they "dance" on the grass.

In fact, "worm charming" is something of a misnomer – "worm alarming" might be more accurate. The practice works because the vibrations roughly mimic the approach of digging moles (which love snacking on the creatures). The worms flee their burrows to avoid the predator, and plop out onto the surface of the ground where they can be readily collected and popped in a bucket.

Bait-gathering fishermen have practiced the technique for a long time, but the first official

World Worm Charming Championships was held in 1980 at a school fair at Willaston County Primary School, in Cheshire. It has been an annual event ever since.

You have a five-minute warm up period, then the clock starts and your three-person team of charmer, catcher and counter sets to work. You can pat, stamp or dance on the ground, but the most successful tactic is to plunge a garden fork approximately 15 cm (5 in.) into the turf and bang it with your hand. This is known locally as "twanging." All worms must be returned to the ground after the contest.

Worm charming is one of those refreshingly open sports that is not dominated by the fastest or strongest athletes – a schoolgirl is as likely to win as a Royal Marine. In 2009, 10-year-old Sophie Smith set the world worm-charming record by raising an incredible 567 worms.

Now, where did I put my entry form?

If you've ever shown a natural talent for pelmanism or the card game "pairs" then perhaps you could become a champion memory athlete. Of course, rather than remembering something as simple as where two cards are, you'll face a slightly stiffer challenge. Like memorizing the exact order of a full pack of fifty-two cards – as fast as you possibly can.

In most physical sports there are very few things you need to remember – which way you're supposed to be running and which goal you're attacking being two of the biggest challenges. But in memory sports, it's ALL mental. There are many types of challenges, but they all involve memorizing a huge amount of information that is presented to you, and then returning it correctly, usually against the clock.

For example, you may be asked to memorize up to fifty words in one minute, with a recall time of four minutes. The current world record is forty-eight words in 59.24 seconds, held by Simon Reinhard from Germany.

One great thing about memory sports is that there is no real barrier to entry. The games are simple to understand, if fiendishly hard to do well. And you can enter the competitive arena by trying a qualifying challenge online. Do well at this and you could eventually make it to the annual World Memory Championships.

It's all in your mind.

There you'll face ten specific challenges:

1. One Hour Numbers
2. Five Minutes Numbers
3. Spoken Numbers, read out one per second
4. Thirty Minutes Binary Digits
5. One Hour Playing Cards
6. Random Lists of Words
7. Names and Faces
8. Five Minutes Historic Dates
9. Abstract Images
10. Speed Cards – Memorize the order of one shuffled deck of fifty-two playing cards as fast as possible.

"After an intense training session [...] I feel visually activated, as if I see the world around myself a bit more clearly."

Simon Reinhard, holder of multiple world memory records

10 | BEARDING

A real growth sport

Men have been proud of their facial hair creations since time immemorial, but modern competitive bearding can be dated to 1990. The Höfener Beard Club organized the first World Beard and Moustache Championships in its hometown of Höfen an der Enz, in Germany's Black Forest. What's the aim of the game? It's simple – grow the most beautifully bushy, luxuriant and sculptured facial hair that you can.

The spectacular creations of the German bearders attracted media attention, and by 1995, beard clubs across northern Europe had hooked up to establish a biennial international competition. In the early years of the twenty-first century, British and American competitors began to challenge the dominance of the Germans, Austrians and Scandinavians, and today a bearding champion can come from anywhere in the world.

Fancy looking facially furry and fabulous? Anyone can become a beardsman – well, as long as you're male and have passed puberty.

Best in show

There are sixteen traditional categories in The World Beard and Moustache Championships (a seventeenth category, the Alaskan Whaler, was added in the 2009 Championships held in Anchorage). These are ordered in three groups: Moustaches, Partial Beards and Full Beards.

Moustaches include the Dali, English and Hungarian styles. Among the Partial Beard designs are the Musketeer, Fu Manchu and Goatee Freestyle. Full Beards offer a wide range of creative options, including the Verdi, Garibaldi – a broad, full and round beard no longer than 20 cm (7.8 in.), Full Beard Natural (usually the most competitive division), and Full Beard Freestyle.

The Full Beard Freestyle division is a chance to show off your creativity as well as your pure hair-growing ability. In 2005, Elmar Weisser from Germany won by sculpting his beard into a hairy representation of the historic Brandenburg Gate.

Select your style

Imperial Moustache   **Muskateer**   **Fu Manchu**   **Full beard Styled Moustache**   **Verdi**   **Garibaldi**

Tips for growing a bigger, better and bushier beard

1 A diet high in protein, plus less stress and more sleep can help make your beard grow faster. Drink lots of water.

2 You may want to consider Biotin, a natural hair-growth supplement that contains important hair-helping vitamins B6, C and E.

3 Commit to growing a beard. Acknowledge that the process takes time. Enjoy all stages of the growth you achieve on the way to your goal.

4 Trim your beard to create the appearance of thicker, fuller hair. Thin and straggly is never a good look.

5 If you have thin, patchy growth, ask your barber for some beard thickener. This can dramatically improve the overall look of your beard.

6 Keep your beard in prime condition. Castor oil is an excellent conditioning treatment to promote growth. Apply it at night and wash off in the morning. You may want to put a towel on your pillow to prevent staining.

Did you know?
The longest beard was
a staggering 5.33 m
(17.5 ft) long.

11 | WELLY WANGING

A welly good idea

In theory, Welly Wanging is a simple sport of distance. You must "wang" (a Yorkshire term meaning to throw) a regulation "welly" (short for Wellington boot, a rubber waterproof boot) as far as possible from a standing or running start. It's like the javelin but with a piece of rubber footwear rather than a deadly weapon.

In a sub-category of the sport you can launch the welly from the end of your foot in the manner of kicking off a pair of shoes. However, the sport has many subtleties that a future world champion should explore.

Booting up a new sport

The Wellington boot is an extremely popular item of footwear in Holmfirth, a rural nook of West Yorkshire. Legend tells of an evening in the misty past when one farmer spilled (accidentally, or perhaps not) some ale into the welly of a fellow yeoman, which was warming by the pub hearth. When this plucky soul rebooted his feet, his socks got a soaking. Fuming, he removed the boot and chased his now-laughing friend out into the night. As the spiller had the fastest legs, the wet-footed farmer was forced to hurl his boot to get his revenge. And thus a new sport was born.

Welly wanging competitions are now held in many countries, but the official World Championships are still held each year in Upperthong in Holmfirth.

Getting the hang of the wang

You must master your wanging technique, and there are four principal styles that you should study:

One handed

The most popular technique. Grasp the upper part of the boot in your fist. Put one foot forward, one back. Extend your arm out behind your back. Launch the boot.

Double handed

Usually done with a shot-putt style circular move to aid momentum.

Between the legs

Children and beginners favor this technique. Face the target, bend your legs and swing the welly up from between your legs.

Backward throw

Like the "Between the legs" style, but with your back to the target. This maximizes the potential backswing, but also increases the chance of the welly flying off target. Or, indeed, straight up in the air and back down onto your head.

Did you know? The maximum run-up allowed is forty-two paces. This honors the author Douglas Adams, a fan of the sport, who posited that the answer to the Ultimate Question of Life, The Universe, and Everything is "42."

Give your championship credentials a kick-start with the ancient Yorkshire art of waterproof-footwear throwing.

WELLY WANG

This makes the sport far more demanding than normal soccer, and the rules have been tweaked to reflect the extra athletic endeavor required:

⚽ Twelve-minute halves – this is to cope with fatigue, and also because after a few minutes it's almost impossible to tell who is on which team

⚽ For a corner, penalty and throw-in, you just drop the ball onto your foot

⚽ No off-side

⚽ 6 a-side, with unlimited squads and substitutions

Dirty players welcomed

If you've ever played footy on a wet January day, you've probably done a bit of swamp soccer already. However, the version of the game pioneered in Finland takes the swampiness angle a few muddy steps further. It's basically like normal soccer, but played on a bog so squelchy that taking a single step is an athletic endeavor, let alone running or making a decent kick.

Better bring a change of clothes

It's not just the goalmouths and the center circle that are slithering patches of churned-up grass and ground. The whole pitch is a bog, with the mud anywhere from 15 to 40 cm (5 to 15 in.) deep.

Has anyone ever called you a filthy tackler? Are you so unfit you feel like you're running in mud?

There are currently an estimated 260 swamp soccer teams around the world. The World Championship is held in Finland every June and the World Cup follows a few weeks later in Scotland.

Even if your team isn't crowned champions, you will still have done your body a big favor. People have been using mud treatments to beautify themselves for centuries, and the effects of swamp soccer are no different. Peel off the muck and you'll be rosy of cheek, firm of limb and bright of eye. Just don't make your mother do your washing...

13 | BEER MILE

Drink a beer, run a quarter mile. Repeat three more times until victorious or rather ill.

Because lager is probably isotonic

The social temptations of university often turn pretty good runners into pretty good drinkers. In many cases, the beer wins out in the end, and that personal-best 1500-m time recedes forever into the mist of schooldays past.

If, however, you are in the happy position of being still pretty handy at both running and drinking, then the Beer Mile is the event for you to make your world championship push. All you have to do is drink four beers while running a mile – sounds simple, but in reality it's one of those "seemed like a good idea at the time" things...

Around and around and around and around

The Beer Mile is run on a standard 400 m track, four-and-a-bit laps of which produce a mile. The competitors line up and wait for starter's orders. The gun is fired, they're off! Not running – downing their first beer. Under the now-standard U.S. rules, this is a 355-ml (12-oz) can of beer. Once the can is dry, it's off for the first full lap around the track. After you have burped and weaved your way around that, your second lap proceeds in the same way, as do the third and fourth. If you vomit at any point you have to run a penalty lap.

41

In Britain, the races are most often run with an imperial pint (20 oz, 568 ml) downed before every lap. This is known as The Queen's Chunder Mile. The current record is 5:08.7.

There are many open competitions and qualifying events, usually held near college campuses. However, the official Beer Mile World Championships was first held in Austin, Texas, in 2014, and that's the event to enter if you want the undisputed title. You'd better get practicing though, as some seriously impressive times have been posted. For years, the great milestone was the five-minute Beer Mile, but this has been recently smashed by some Roger Bannister-like boozers. In 2015, Lewis Kent, 21, set a phenomenal men's world record of 4:47.17. His beer of choice was Amsterdam Blonde.

Did you know? The Beer Mile has been developed into other running and drinking events, including the 4 x 4 Beer Relay, the Beer 2 Mile and the 3,000-m Vodka Steeplechase.

Conditioning is everything

Many Olympic competitors head overseas for their pre-event training, and Germany, Austria and Switzerland are ideal places to go for your athletic and alcohol-based Beer Mile conditioning. These countries have a tradition of *Kastenlauf* (short for "Bierkastenlauf"), which translates as "beer-crate running." In this race, two-person teams must run around a 10-km (6.2-mile) course carrying a crate of beer, the contents of which they must consume before the finish line. This may boost your stamina, both in your legs and your head.

Above: Young men run around Maschsee Lake with a crate of beer in Hanover, Germany.

14 | OUTHOUSE RACING

WHERE NEVADA, U.S.
SINCE 1990

Flush with success

We've heard of porta potties, but this is ridiculous. The world outhouse racing championship in Virginia City, Nevada, is a team race for tiny-wheeled toilets.

The commode contest owes its existence to a local county ban on all outdoor plumbing, presumably enacted in the name of progress. However, the outhouse owners of Virginia City were outraged, and they promptly paraded their privies along the town's main street as a protest against the ordinance.

The annual world championship race itself takes place at high noon and runs down C Street, the town's main drag. Your team must build and decorate its own outhouse and you must adorn yourselves in eye-catching costumes. One person takes the hot seat and the remaining team members then push, pull or drag the outhouse as fast as they can. First outhouse to break the toilet paper finish line is the WC (world champ).

Tactical tip

A glance at the podium placers in 2015 will show you that a toilet-themed team name is one essential ingredient of success:

 Sport A Potty

 Dung Fo Warrior

 Commando Comode

 Storm Pooper

OUTHOUSE RACES OCT. 6-7

267

BUCKET OF BLOOD
SINCE 1876
SALOON
VIRGINIA CITY NEVADA
Famous The World Over

The *pièce de résistance* of peripatetic plumbing.

Did you know? Virginia City was one of Nevada's many mining boomtowns. More than $400 million in gold and silver was dug from beneath its dusty soil — that would be worth around $20 billion today.

Have you got the titanium tongue it takes to be crowned "King of the Sting"?

A rash choice of sports

Nettle tea is rather nice. Nettle wine is passable. But actually eating raw stinging nettles straight from the hedgerow? That's another thing entirely.

We all know nettles hurt, but why they hurt is rather impressive. Every leaf of *urtica dioica* bristles with thousands of microscopic hairs that function as detachable needles. They are not only prickly, but they spike a nasty mix of irritants into any fleshy unfortunate that rubs against them.

Enter the World Nettle Eating Championship and you'll sit down to a dinner table piled high with 51-cm (20-in.) segments of cut stinging nettle plants. You'll then have one hour to strip from the stalk as many stinging leaves as you can, and eat them. You have to scoff standard competition nettles, not a less-vicious strain you have found in a corner of your garden, and you can't load yourself up with painkillers. Your only solace is a swig of beer (or water, if you have to).

Taking pains to prepare

Like many sports that are on the silly side, competitive nettle eating has its origins in a pub. Back in the 1980s, Alex Williams, a local farmer, was letting off steam to a friend about the ferocious nettles in his fields. He had measured one at 4.72 m (15.5 ft) tall, and if any man could show him a bigger brute, why, he'd eat his stinging monster himself! His pal sipped, nodded, and soon toddled off to bed. The next day

he returned with a nettle from his own farm that was 4.88 m (16 ft) long. Williams was true to his word. He chomped the nettle down, and so the World Nettle Eating Championship was born.

To win this world championship you need skill, appetite, and most of all a masochistic ability to withstand needless pain. Because it can hurt. A lot. If you want to avoid most of the agony, it pays to study the technique of former champions. You need

to deftly fold the nettle leaves over to press the hairs together. Then squish the leaves into compact balls and flip them straight to your back teeth. Mash them with your molars and gulp them down the hatch touching as little tongue, gum or throat as possible.

If you're good, you will avoid any stings while savoring a little of the plant's flavor – a cross between spinach and rocket. Don't savor the deliciousness too long; remember, you're in a race.

Phil Thorne from Colyton, Devon, is the world-record holder. In 2014, he polished off an astonishing 24 m (80 ft) of nettles, 5.5 m (18 ft) more than his nearest rival.

16 | MOBILE PHONE THROWING

It's just a shame you're not allowed to throw it at someone.

WHERE FINLAND | **SINCE** 2000
FIRST PRIZE A NEW MOBILE PHONE

This call is over

The organizers of this wonderful world championship have kindly let us reproduce their credo here:

> Mobile Phone Throwing is light [*sic*] and modern Finnish sport that suits for people [*sic*] of all ages. It combines recycling philosophy and fun spirit in active sport. A part of the philosophy is also a spiritual freedom from being available all the time.

Doesn't that instantly make you want to take part? It taps into a very common love/hate relationship that we have with our phones. And that love/hate feeling is perfectly captured in this event where you simply have to hurl a device of your choice as far as possible.

Mobile phones facilitate our modern lives. The device is an amazing invention that puts a computer in your pocket and makes the people you care about available anywhere and anytime. But who hasn't run out of battery while explaining a late arrival to a loved one? Or texted an embarrassingly auto-corrected message to their mother-in-law? Or been beaten at Angry Birds by a 5-year-old girl?

In situations like these, the temptation to hurl your very expensive supercomputer into the nearest river is all too real. Luckily, the Mobile Phone Throwing World Championships gives you the chance to unleash your locomotive communication frustration. You'll need to practice channelling your anger into athletic action – the world record for the longest throw is 97.73 m (320.6 ft). That's as long as a soccer field.

It's worth remembering that Finnish company Nokia pioneered mobile phone technology and by 1998 was the largest manufacturer in the world. The fact that it was knocked from its perch by the iPhone, and almost went bankrupt, perhaps contributes to the high performance levels of Finns in this event.

Did you know?
The Cray-2 was the world's fastest supercomputer until 1990, clocking 1.9 GFLOPS (billion calculations per second). It was the size of a washing machine. An iPhone 6 clocks 115.2 GFLOPS.

17 | TREE CLIMBING

Scaling the heights of sporting glory

Tree-climbing championships began in California as a way for professional arborists to learn rescue skills, try new climbing techniques and check out the latest equipment. Frankly, it also gave them an excellent opportunity to do a bit of high-level showing off.

First up are the preliminary rounds, where the tree-climbing competitors must take part in five different events: Aerial Rescue, Work Climb, Secured Footlock, Belayed Speed Climb and Throwline. Each climber is judged and scored for their efforts and the highest total wins. The few best climbers to make it through qualifying then compete in the Masters' Challenge. This single event is scored on technique and skill and will decide the ultimate male and female world champions.

High standards

Competitive tree climbing is a potentially dangerous sport, and so the strictest safety standards must be adhered to at all times. This means that the event is only open to members of the International Society of Arboriculture. Guest climbers are occasionally invited if they excel at an event that is recognized by the ISA.

Before committing yourself to joining the ranks of professional arborists, you could perhaps take yourself off to Indonesia and try your hand (and feet) at one of the world's other great tree-climbing events.

In the Areca Tree Climbing Festival, competitors have to scale a 10-m (33-ft) high, very thin and branchless Areca tree that has also been deliberately greased. This is very, very hard to do. To motivate you towards success, you'll find a selection of presents, including household hardware, food and bicycles at the top of the trunk as rewards should you make it up there.

Unleash your inner squirrel and you could make it to the top!

18 | EXTREME IRONING

WHERE ENGLAND, GERMANY | **SINCE** 2002 | **USEFUL EQUIPMENT** ANTI-GRAVITY BOOTS
ESSENTIAL EQUIPMENT IRON, IRONING BOARD, STARCH

Under pressure

Ironing can be hard enough when you're late for work and you forgot to take your shirts out of the washing machine. But that's nowhere near hardcore enough for the international-standard competitors of Extreme Ironing. To partake in the sport you simply have to do your ironing somewhere incredibly dangerous. But to be world champ? Well, you must take your board somewhere very risky indeed AND smooth out your laundry in an impressively neat way. It is, according to the Extreme Ironing Bureau, a "danger sport that combines the thrills of an extreme outdoor activity with the satisfaction of a well-pressed shirt."

The sport lends itself very well to freestyling – all you really need is an ironing board and a bit of gravity and the rest is up to you. That's how it started out, with eccentric Brits doing their laundry chores in some seriously deranged locations. Since then, extreme ironers have been spotted doing their thing atop precipitous mountains, while parachuting, under the ice of a frozen lake and on the northbound lane of the M1 motorway (a very, very busy English freeway).

The first world championships took place in 2002 in Bavaria, Germany, with twelve teams representing ten nations. (The ever-smart Brits put in three teams.) If you decide to enter the next championships, you need to be aware that you'll be judged on your creative ironing skills as well as the sharpness of your folds. Plus, you have to step up to the crease in the five categories described on page 55.

If Spiderman were real, he'd win this sport hands down and feet up.

World championship categories

Water – river rapids would be the natural enemy of ironing, but you can use a surfboard or a canoe to help you stay dry.

Urban – for example, ironing on top of a broken-down car.

Forest – the squirrels will be very surprised when you get your starch out in the upper branches of a large sycamore.

Rocky – here you must clamber up a specially built climbing wall.

Freestyle – knock the judges' socks off however you see fit. Just make sure you give them a quick press afterwards.

Did you know? The very first extreme ironer was Phil Shaw, of Leicester, England. He came home from a hard day's work one evening in 1997 and, to unwind, decided he'd head out to go rock climbing. However, he also saw that he had a huge pile of ironing to do before the next morning. Phil simply decided to combine the two activities, and so a thrilling new sport was born.

Psychological superiority

You may think that Rock, Paper, Scissors is the very definition of a random game. On the count of three you form your hand into your chosen symbol. Rock crushes Scissors, Scissors cut Paper, and Paper wraps Rock, so you instantly have either a win or a stalemate and you play again. The first person to an agreed number of wins is the overall champ. But how can you know what your opponent is about to play from one of these three very basic moves?

Well, it *should* be a random game, but it turns out that humans are terrible at being truly random, and there are several psychological tactics that you can use to play better.

If you're up against a novice player, throw a lot of Paper. Why? In championship circles there's a phrase, "Rock is for rookies." New players throw a lot of Rocks, thinking it looks forceful, decisive and, well, manly. So your Paper will soon wrap up that match.

Conversely, if your opponent is experienced enough to know "Rock is for rookies," then you throw Scissors, knowing he'll throw a lot of early Paper, thinking that YOU are the rookie.

Throw the move that would have lost to your opponent's last throw. Flustered and novice players will often subconsciously throw the move that beat their last one. If your

opponent threw Scissors last time, this time they are likely to throw Rock. So you play Paper, which would have lost to them last time, but now will win.

Watch for two-in-a-row. New players don't want to seem predictable and think that making the same throw three times in a row is a sign of predictability. They may make two identical throws one after the other, but are unlikely to make three.

If you don't know what to throw next, throw Paper. Statistically, it is thrown the least often in competitions – 29.6 percent of the time. The average would be 33.33 percent, so it is 3.73 percent less common than your opponent might think.

Speech play. Announce what you are going to throw and then deliver exactly that. Why? Chances are, your opponent won't think you're bold enough to actually do that. If you say you're going to throw Rock, they won't think, "I'd better throw Paper, then." So you can discount that throw, and your Rock will have a 50 percent chance of victory rather than a 33.3 percent chance.

The first world championship was held in a Toronto bar in 2002. The bar owners thought a couple of dozen of their friends might try their hands, but hundreds of keen throwers turned up to compete and by 2006 the world championship title was being battled for in Las Vegas, for a $50,000 prize.

If you get really good, you can move onto...

Rock-Paper-Scissors-Spock-Lizard

Rock-Paper-Scissors-Spock-Lizard is an expanded version of the game with five possible plays. "Spock" (the Star Trek Vulcan salute) and "Lizard" (imagine your hand is inside a sock puppet) are added to the three basic moves. Spock smashes Scissors and vaporizes rock; he is poisoned by Lizard and disproven by Paper. Lizard poisons Spock and eats Paper; it is crushed by Rock and decapitated by Scissors.

You've got to hand it to the champion of this game.

"Sometimes the smallest things take up the most room in your heart."

Winnie-the-Pooh

Go with the flow

You have to love a sport where a 110-kg (243-lb) professional rugby player has about the same chance of becoming world champion as a 6-year-old boy. Less, probably, because the 6-year-old boy will have been doing a bit more practicing in his daily life. Pooh sticks was first played by Winnie-the-Pooh and Christopher Robin in *The House at Pooh Corner*, by A. A. Milne. All you need is a bridge over a river and

then rush over to the downstream side to see whose stick comes out first. Repeat until you are called in for your tea.

The world championship has been held at Day's Lock on the River Thames, since 1984. This is one of the very best places in the world for whiling away an afternoon playing this sport. Eight competitors are each given a different colored stick to make judging easier, and the winner of each heat goes through to

> **"You have to watch the other rounds to see which stick is fastest. I picked the yellow stick. That's the best."**
>
> Charlie Roman, aged 7,
> World Pooh Sticks Champion 2016

The winning formula

Do you need to practice to be in with a chance? Or is it all just the luck of the landing? Well, Dr Rhys Morgan, from the Royal Academy of Engineering, has calculated a formula to maximize your chances of being crowned champ:

PP (Perfect Pooh stick) = A x I x Cd

A = Cross-sectional area. A larger area creates more drag, which means your stick will get caught more by the current.

I = Density. Ideally, your stick should be weighty enough to sink just under the surface of the water, away from any wind.

Cd = Drag coefficient. The stick's shape and roughness. Go for as rough as possible, with lots of sticky-out bits of bark.

21 | PIG SQUEALING

Snout – check, trotters – check, comedy curly tail – check. Ok, on your marks, get set, OINK!

WHERE FRANCE | **SINCE** 1975
WHY NO ONE IS SURE

Could you be the pig of the bunch?

Do pigs in France oink in a French accent? That's something you might like to ask yourself if you enter "Le Championnat de France du Cri de Cochon," the Pig-Squealing Championships. Because to be a winner you'll have to squeal like a pig in as realistic a way as possible. It's just one of the many porcine pastimes you can enjoy as part of "La Pourcailhade," the Festival of the Pig, which is held every August in the town of Trie-sur-Baïse, southwestern France. There are pig-related exhibits, pig races, eating contests (presumably involving sausages) and other competitions.

Makin' bacon

So you've decided to give championship pig-imitating a shot. Well, you can't just stand up on stage and squeal. The audience takes this sport *très sérieusement*. First, you need a decent pig costume. You need to move in a pig-like way. Plus, not only do the noises you produce have to be authentically piggish, they also have to mimic the sounds made at various stages of a pig's life. A piglet does not sound like a mature porker. Exactly when a pig's voice breaks is something you will have to research as part of your preparations.

If you need further tips on squealing like a pig, you might want to ask Ned Beatty...

22 | MUGGLE QUIDDITCH

You'll need to deliver a magical performance

To many observers, quidditch was a bafflingly chaotic game in the Harry Potter movies and books that required, as an absolutely essential item of kit, a fully working magical broomstick. The fact that such a piece of sporting equipment does not really exist hasn't stopped some athletic muggles from setting up a full quidditch league and World Cup competition.

Quidditch is a 7-a-side, co-ed contact sport that blends aspects of several games, including rugby, dodgeball and tag. Players must have a broom between their legs at all times.

You can play in one of four positions: seeker, beater, chaser, keeper. There is also the snitch, an anthropomorphized version of the golden-winged ball in the movies.

The snitch wears yellow kit and has a Velcro tail. Catching him or her is worth thirty points.

To make it to the World Cup you'll need to join an active team and secure victory in the regional qualifying rounds. Make it through and you'll be one of eighty sides gathering at the world's premier competition for the honor of being crowned world champions.

The team

Seeker
Chases after the snitch and grabs the Velcro tail hanging from the snitch's shorts to score points and end the game.

Chasers
Score goals with the quaffle by throwing or kicking it into the hoops.

Beaters
Use the bludgers to disrupt other players.

Keeper
Guards the hoops from opposing chasers.

The balls

Snitch

Quaffle

Bludgers

You don't need to be a wizard to play a sport that is really taking off.

23 | WINTER SWIMMING

WHERE FINLAND, RUSSIA | **SINCE** 2005
ESSENTIAL EQUIPMENT A LITTLE EXTRA BODY FAT WON'T GO AMISS

Making a splash

Having the local lake freeze over might seem to put an end to your open-water swimming season, but that's just the *start* of the fun if you're a competitive winter swimmer.

As a sport, winter or ice swimming was pioneered by the tough-as-nails Finns. Jumping into icy waters was something that they had simply done

for personal pleasure. But now there are also major competitions in Belarus, Sweden and Russia – the 2016 world championship was held in Siberia.

A swimming area is hacked out of ice thick enough to hold a snowmobile. The air temperature is very, very sub-zero. Helpers stand by with nets to fish out any pesky bits of ice that begin forming in the pool. Crowds dressed in down jackets, snow boots and

woolly hats gather to watch the action. There are several distance events and age classes, including junior and veteran events.

It might seem absolutely crazy, but as sports go, it's certainly invigorating – does anything compare with diving into Arctic waters for delivering a jolt of adrenaline? After their races all the competitors emerge smiling, laughing and full of life. Now it's time for a lengthy and well-earned soak in the hot tub and perhaps a warming vodka.

How to brave the icy waters

You will need to do several months of training in open-water swimming to acclimatize your body before attempting an ice swim. Such training can seem daunting, but there are several steps you can take to unleash your inner penguin:

1 Dive on in. The trick to acclimatizing quickly is mental. Tell yourself you know it's going to be cold and embrace that feeling.

2 Exhale when you enter the water. Your ribcage automatically contracts with the cold, which makes inexperienced swimmers feel they can't breathe. By exhaling, your first breath will come naturally.

3 Wait a moment. You might be thinking "this is awful," but your body will soon react and give you a nice thrill.

4 Set out for a target rock or other marker. With a goal in sight, your motivation and circulation will improve.

5 Don't be afraid to yell a bit! Some shouting, grunting and "oh-my-Lording" will help you get fired up and moving on your cold-water swim.

Are you ready to take the polar bear plunge?

Masters of the marsh

A vast mire stretches out towards the horizon. A sloppy amalgam of brown, acidic water and decayed plant material. Chill, clinging mist lurks above the saturated ground. This is not your average athletics venue. But then bog snorkellers are not your average athletes.

They race up and down a 55-m (180-ft) trench cut into a peat bog, against the clock. A snorkel, flippers and perhaps a silly costume are their only aids against the cold and the mud.

Can you swim like an eel, while avoiding the leeches?

"Buoyancy, and an ability to pick the racing path through the reeds."

A competitor, on what it takes to be a champion bog snorkeller

This craziness began back in 1976 when regulars in The Neuadd Arms in the tiny Welsh town of Llanwrtyd Wells were talking deep into the night about how to raise funds for a local charity. In their ale-inspired wisdom they decided that they should head up onto the local mire and swim through its murk.

Dive on in

Although the race takes place in a water-filled trench, it isn't a flat-out swimming contest. Clumps of reeds, lumps of peat and kinks in the trench demand a more versatile technique. The current world champion,

Kirsty Johnson, used butterfly kick to the end of the course, front crawl after the turn and a final burst of butterfly to finish in her extraordinary time of 1 minute 22.56 seconds.

Before heading to the world championships, you could get some practice in some of the other bog snorkelling events that take place in Ireland, Wales, Australia and Sweden. If you get good, you could also try your flippers at the bog-snorkelling triathlon and the even more improbable mountain-bike bog snorkelling race.

Watch the feathers fly

A long steel pole shines in the July sun. It stretches across a pit of water, murky and brown. Two flit-eyed competitors stand at the pole's ends. They climb onto the smooth metal cylinder, straddling it between their legs. Inch by inch they shuffle out into the center, to face each other above the water. For several unblinking seconds they eye each other in silence. Then, at a shouted command, they pull pillows from behind their backs and try to batter each other into a splashy oblivion.

You may have smashed your younger brother into fits of giggles when you were kids, but you'll need more than a longer reach to triumph on the pillow-fighting world stage in Sonoma County, CA. Balance, technique, a good grip and lightning speed are all essential if you're to avoid a watery walk back to the losers' field. So give it your all, and at least you'll sleep well when your head hits the pillow tonight.

Even if you lose,
at least you'll
have something
to cry into.

TERMITE & PEST
CONTROL, INC.
707-526-6055

Fancy footwork

A kick in the shins is usually just an unpleasant accident that sometimes happens in a game of soccer. It's not the kind of move you'd base an entire sport on. Unless, that is, you're some tough-as-nails seventeenth-century English miners.

As if working down a tin mine wasn't hard enough, they decided that they would amuse themselves in what little spare time they had by putting on their heaviest steel-toe boots, grabbing each other by the collar and trying to kick each other in the shins so hard that their opponent fell over in agony.

Unbelievably, this torture – sorry, sport – grew in popularity and spread throughout the country. By the 1850s it was one of the most popular events in the Cotswold Olimpick Games, an eccentric English forerunner of the modern Olympic Games. Since the Olimpicks were revived in 1966, shin kicking has once again proven to be insanely popular. And just plain insane.

The rules

All shin kickers wear white coats that represent traditional shepherds' smocks and which have a sturdy collar for grappling with. With your opponent in hand, you can start kicking him. As well as cracking his shin with your toe, you can also try to swipe his leg from the side. You are permitted to stuff straw in front of your shins as padding to lessen the pain. But it will still hurt. When the agony gets too much, you must shout out "sufficient," which is the shin-kicking safe word, and that concedes the match. Alternatively, a winner is declared when he manages to boot his rival so hard that he drops to the deck and starts groaning.

To ensure that the bodily assault is done in a fair manner, each match is overseen by an umpire, known as a Stickler.

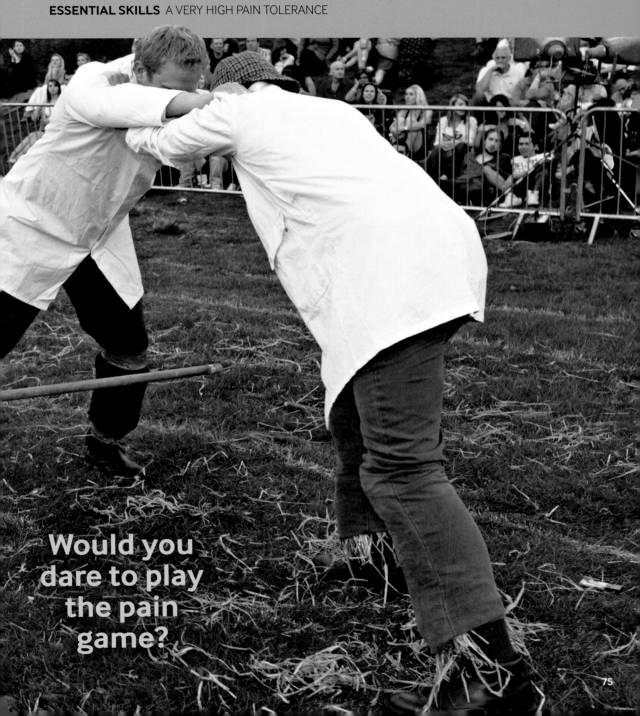

Would you
dare to play
the pain
game?

75

How to be a champ

"It actually takes a great tolerance of pain, but you need to be agile and you need to be fit. It sounds like it's just a rough up, but it's not, it's actually quite skillful."

Graham Greenall, event chairman

Probably your biggest competitive advantage is simply having a screw loose. After all, the early shin kickers were reputed to have built pain tolerance by hitting their own shins with hammers.

"It's basically just having the will to do what the other man won't, to be honest. To keep standing taking a kick."

Ben Greenall, event Stickler

27 | LATTE ART

WHERE WORLDWIDE | **SINCE** 2006
ESSENTIAL SKILLS STEADY HANDS, SHARP EYES

A competition
worth getting
all steamed
up about.

Bean there, done that

If your coffee is taking forever to arrive, don't berate your barista – it could be that they are in training for the world Latte Art Championship.

Being a champion latte artist is all about creating beautiful designs in coffee froth. It's certainly a tricky medium to work in – you have to move surely and swiftly before the foam loses its volume and becomes just another cup of joe.

The world championship starts with a preliminary round where the competitors produce one original latte design. For the main event you have to make two identical free-pour lattes and two identical designer lattes. Your five scores are totalled and the top six entrants go through to the final round. This is where the heat is really on. You have to make two identical free-pour macchiatos, two identical free-pour lattes, and two identical designer-patterned lattes.

All your pours will be assessed on visual attributes, creativity, identical patterns in the pairs, contrast in patterns and overall performance. This final round is winner takes all – the top score here will earn you the title of World Latte Art Champion.

This is a truly international competition, with entrants from dozens of countries descending on Shanghai in 2016 to prove their worth in froth. If you've been impressed by a simple heart or coffee bean design on your cappuccino, prepare to be amazed by the standard on show here. Swans, snowflakes and even landscapes are all brought into swirling, short-lived existence.

Top-class competitors all have their own personal milk jugs to create a truly precise pour. Many of them use toothpicks and straws to etch designs into the foam, as well as food coloring to add a splash of life to their creations.

"[It's about] being calm and focused on steaming the milk first of all. And having a clear vision of what you want to pour before executing it."
Competitor Ian Chagunda, on the secret to making great latte art

Do you have what it takes to be a rock star?

Stone free

Layered skyscrapers that defy gravity. A single harmonious arch built from stones of many sizes. A chunk of granite stands on one improbable corner. Rocks as smooth as eggs are stacked in perfect stillness.

Rock stacking has been an activity for as long as people have whiled away a lazy afternoon by a river. It's also one of our newest competitive sports thanks to the World Rock Stacking Championship.

How will you stack up?

All you have to do is build a pile of rocks in a remarkable or beautiful way. No glue or cement is allowed and your only tools are your bare hands. The competition has four categories: tallest stack, best balancing rock, best rock arch, and the most artistic rock stack design.

Part art, part meditation, part construction, rock stacking is a unique and mindful way to create something beautiful. You will need focus and calmness. And because it is inevitable that the wind, rain or a passing lizard will cause your creation to tumble, you must acknowledge the pastime's ephemeral nature if you want to excel.

"I think people have been stacking rocks since people were people. It's a great mind cleaner. If you're thinking about the bill that was late or your girlfriend, it's not going to work."

David Allen, a professional rock stacker
from Maine

29 | AIR GUITAR

For those who
are about to
rock...

Did you know? Air Guitar is about more than crowd-wowing showmanship.
The official championships also extol the wider benefits of performances:
"The purpose of the Air Guitar World Championships is to promote
world peace [...] wars would end, climate change stop and all bad
things disappear, if all the people in the world played the Air Guitar."

Welcome to the jungle

You get up from your seat and climb the steps. Turn to face the crowd. Nod to the judges. Shake your hands to loosen your fingers. Double check your Les Paul and leap into imaginary action...

Air Guitar is all about showing off your musical expertise with an instrument that isn't actually there. Your air guitar can be acoustic or electric. It could be six-string, twelve-string or have more than one neck. However, you are NOT allowed to play air drums, air keyboards or, indeed, air tambourine.

Learn from the best

Jimmy Page, Slash, Eric Clapton, Jimi Hendrix, Eddie Van Halen, Brian May – it's their technique, energy and sheer showmanship that you must channel if you are going to be crowned world champ. Luckily this is one strange pastime that you can start practicing right now, in the comfort of your own home. Simply fire up a playlist, climb on your bed and start rocking out.

In the world championships you must successfully perform in two sixty-second rounds. In the first you play a song or medley of your choice. The second-round song selection is made by the organizers and is usually kept secret – improvisation is everything!

Your efforts will be scored from 4.0 to 6.0 in the following **four categories**:

Technical merit – how much did your performance look like real playing? Were your riffs, chords and solos discernible and accurate?

Mimesmanship – did you create the illusion of there being an actual invisible guitar in your hands?

Stage presence – did you have the charisma of a real rock star?

Airness – how awesome and empowering was your performance as a work of art?

Lofty ambitions

Most of us made paper planes in elementary school, so surely becoming world champ of such a sport is child's play? Not exactly. You'll need more than a few folds and a neat follow-through to make the world stage. The triennial airplane championship was first held in 2006, and by 2015 the event was pulling in contestants from eighty-six countries from around the world. You'll need to enter one of the hundreds of national competitions to join the world's finest folio flyers next time around.

You can be world champion in three categories: distance flown, longest hangtime and aerobatics, where you have to throw your plane in the most stylish way possible. Your plane's design should be very different for each event.

How to get big air

Brains and brawn, basically. If you are creating an original paper plane design, it pays to study a little aeronautical theory to create your aircraft. It's no coincidence that Veselin Ivanov, distance champion in 2015, is an engineer by trade. You'll also need a good arm: the current world record distance throw of 69.14 m (226.8 ft) was made by quarterback Joe Ayoob with a plane designed by expert folder John Collins.

"I think after the first throw in the pre-elimination with 47 meters I was kind of happy but I knew I could throw more."

Veselin Ivanov, Bulgarian engineer and world champion

If you want to be a champ, you need to aim high.

Fold your way to success

Here's how to fold your very own model of the world record-breaking paper plane that flew 69.14 m (226.8 ft). Designed by John Collins, it is nicknamed the "Suzanne."

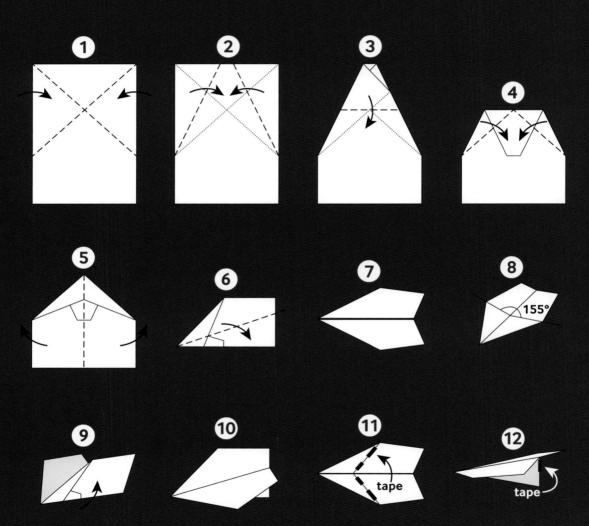

Shear class

If you have ever taken a set of hair clippers to your own head and been impressed with the result, maybe you have what it takes to make it as a champion sheep shearer. All you have to do is apply your skills to a large animal that really doesn't want to be sheared, against the clock and without missing patches or nicking the animal's skin.

Welcome to the Wimbledon of sheep shearing – the Golden Shears in New Zealand. It's hardly surprising that competitive shearing was born here; this country has the highest density of sheep in the world – forty million sheep to only four million people.

Where there's a wool there's a way

You can choose from categories that use traditional hand shears or electric cutters to take off the fleece. You'll need a good shearing strategy to de-wool your sheep – beginners usually start with the *Bowen Technique*, but with the more advanced *Tally-Hi* method the sheep struggle less and the shearer can move up to thirty seconds faster per animal.

First up are the two qualifying heats where you will have to shear at least five sheep per round. The fastest six times recorded here will qualify for the final, in which the world's six greatest shearers face each other in a shear-off. Each shearer has to clip twenty sheep against the clock, with penalty points added for missing any areas of wool. The world record of 15 minutes 27.4 seconds – more than a sheep-a-minute – was set in 2003.

How to get good

Technique and practice are all. Head on down to your local sheep farm and ask if you can lend a hand. Alternatively you could get a job in a dog-grooming parlor and work your way up from there.

The competition

If you do make it to the finals, you could find yourself up against the legendary David Fagan. This New Zealand sheep shearer has won the Golden Shears contest a record sixteen times and holds ten world records. He's a truly fearsome competitor, so if you do lose to him there's no need to bleat about it...

Giving animals haircuts against the clock.

Sole ambition

When he was a young boy, Alistair King wanted to be a motocross world champion. That adrenaline-fuelled ambition didn't work out, but his competitive fire still burned hotly, and in 2015 he became a world champion in a different field – shoe mending.

The Shoe Service Institute of America has held an annual convention for the last 112 years, at which it celebrates the skills of the world's finest shoe repairers.

Alistair, 29, from Crewkerne in Wiltshire, England, rose through the British repairing ranks to become national champion before walking away with the world title.

You have to be first with your last.

Patented technique

The competition rules demand repairs to two pairs of shoes: one pair of ladies' shoes and one men's pair using a leather half sole and heel. You must replicate the original shoe as closely as possible. It's done against the clock, so you have to repair swiftly as well as surely.

"I borrowed a pair of my wife Sophie's light-tan Loake brogues from a shelf under the stairs and I bought a pair of black Oliver Sweeney Aldeburgh brogues with worn-out soles on eBay for £90. It was a very technical repair – but I'm still getting over the 72-hour party."

Alistair King, world champion 2015

A spine-crushing, thigh-straining race to get into the record books.

I be faster than thee

It's hardly reassuring that the World Coal Carrying Championship is sponsored by an undertaker. Specifically, an undertaker going by the name of Mr. Box. The sport is hard enough without such worrying additional details: you have to carry a bag of coal weighing a whopping 50 kg (112 lb) around a 1 km-long urban racecourse.

The event takes place in Gawthorpe in northern England, in the heart of what was once a busy mining area. It has its origins in a bet between two coal delivery men in the Beehive pub as to who was the fastest and strongest. They duly downed their ales and went outside to prove the matter.

Running the race

Getting the gargantuan bag up onto your shoulders isn't the hard part, as a strapping coal merchant will lift it straight from his flatbed truck onto the shoulders of all competitors just behind the start line.

Nor is it too tricky to support the bag's weight. Moving with it, however, is another thing entirely. Having such a huge weight on your shoulders

radically alters the height of your center of gravity. If the coal moves away from the center line of your body then, like a felled tree, it really, really wants to topple and it's nearly impossible to stop that topple once it has started.

Key coal-carrying strategies

One important tip is to wiggle a lump of coal into the two corners of the bag before you start. These improvised "toggles" will allow you to take a commanding grip of the bag. You should also smash the body of the bag a bit to loosen the coal so that you can form it around your neck into a sort of collar, rather than a single lump. Picture a shepherd carrying a sheep over his shoulders, holding the animal's legs in either hand.

A further challenge is that with your head and shoulders weighed down, it is rather difficult to see where you are going. The best thing is to simply follow

the heels of the person in front of you or, if you fall adrift of the pack, echolocate your racing line between the cheering and rather beery crowds. Should you veer seriously off course or drop your coal sack, stewards are standing by to get you back on track.

After a minute or so your lower back will begin to burn. Rather than slow down to lessen this pain, your best bet is now to speed up: it's going to hurt from here on out and you might as well get the agony over

The world record is a frankly astonishing 4 minutes 6 seconds – a pretty good time for running the distance even without the weight of an average 15-year-old boy on your back. The winner of the veterans' race confessed that he had been running around his local park for the last few weeks carrying a bag of coal that weighed 64 kg (140 lb). Compared with that, he said, this race was a doddle.

Right: Josie, a Chinese Crested owned by Linda Elmquist from Tucson, Arizona, before the start of the annual 2014 World's Ugliest Dog Contest at the Sonoma-Marin Fair in Petaluma, California.

Looking ruff

If you've got it, flaunt it. Not style or beauty, but pure low-down ugliness, of the canine variety. That's what the World's Ugliest Dog Championships are all about – whose pooch is the least pulchritudinous.

We're talking crossed eyes, straggly hair, oversized tongues, crooked teeth and, indeed, all these features at once.

Before you object to the nature of such a contest, it really isn't as if the dogs are in any way offended at being paraded for their foulness. They love the attention, and their owners clearly love them.

Plus, if you do decide to enter this world championship, you'll be heading to the cat and dog shelter and taking home some poor wonky-eyed woofer that no one else wants. Which is simply wonderful of you. Good luck!

You don't need any talent at all to win this world championship, just a willing and horrible hound.

Did you know? In 2015, the world champion was a dog appropriately named Quasi Modo. This crossbreed has a shortened spine that makes him look more like a hyena than a dog. Quasi Modo "epitomized excellence in ugliness," according to chief judge Brian Sobel.

Gone fishin' – sort of

There are lots of fishing competitions out there, but they can be very disappointing if those pesky fish decide not to bite. So here's an angling world championship where success is entirely within your hands – fly-casting.

In this sport, you don't have to catch a fish at all. You simply have to be accurate or lengthy with the cast of your fishing rod. You could practice this event in your back yard, if it's long enough!

The world championship brings together the best fly-casters from around the world to compete in six different events: trout accuracy, trout distance, sea-trout distance, salmon distance and two separate Spey distances of 4.6 m (15.1 ft) and 5.5 m/4.89 m (18 ft/16 ft).

If the fish aren't biting, you can still be winning.

Troutstanding accuracy

The trout accuracy event is very popular and demands great skill. There are four targets, each of which has three rings measuring 60 cm, 120 cm and 180 cm (23.6 in., 47.2 in. and 70.9 in.) in diameter. These targets are placed at random positions between 8 and 15 m (26 – 49 ft) from the casting stand. You must cast using a #5 weight line and your rod can be no longer than 2.75 m (9 ft). You make sixteen casts (four on each target) and can score a maximum of eighty points. Even if you don't win, you can still tell all your friends about the cast that got away...

Stadium waves

Rescuing someone from a tragic drowning in tempestuous waves is heroic in itself. But to do so against dozens of other competitors – and an ever-ticking clock – makes you a true champion of world lifesaving.

The International Lifesaving Federation was founded in 1910 with the noble mission of saving lives in the aquatic environment. Its motto of "fit to save a life" encourages the skills, strength and stamina that are needed to help pluck the unlucky from amid deadly waves. These admirable abilities are celebrated at its biennial world championships.

Several events are held in the swimming pool, including obstacle races, manikin-carrying races and swimming medleys. More dramatic are the events on the open ocean. Currents and waves can make these races unpredictable and you'll need experience, tactics and endurance if you are to triumph. A trendy swim cap is also essential.

There are running races on the beach and races into the surf – for example, the Ocean Man and Ocean Woman competition. In this you must complete a 1.2-km (0.75-mile) course that includes a swim leg, a board leg, a surf ski leg and a beach-sprint finish. There are also team races, relays, youth events and the spectacular surfboat race, where teams pull their rescue boat out into heavy swell as fast as they can.

Perhaps the most exciting races are the simulated rescues. Rather than wait for lots of people to start simultaneously drowning (which might be a Health and Safety issue), competitive lifesavers must swim out and retrieve a manikin.

The Lifesaving World Championships take place every two years and attract up to 5,000 competitors and officials for fourteen days of events. All those fit bodies probably draw quite a few spectators, too.

Become a champ
and a better
human being at
the same time.

It all starts with roadkill.

Life after death

The US Open tennis and British Open golf tournaments are, in reality, far from open. They are nowadays contested by the most elite professionals. But there is an arena where any amateur, however humble, can put their work up to be judged alongside that of the most seasoned professionals in the world championships. Your only qualification standard is that you must have stripped the skin from a dead animal, treated its hide and reformed it into a lifelike simulacrum of its once-vital self.

This is the lively sport of competitive taxidermy, whose world championship features eighteen categories to further widen your chance of success. These include a Youth Division, a Collective Artists Division (where more than one taxidermist worked on the entry) and the Live Taxidermy Sculpture Division (thankfully this doesn't involve the stuffing of live animals, but the creation of a taxidermy piece within twenty-four hours). In 2015 there was an impressive total of $42,000 worth of prizes on offer, as well as the honor of being named the world's premier animal mounter.

So next time you hit a rabbit with your car don't leave the carcass on the road; take it home and do something artistic with it instead.

You can also try

If taxidermy is a little too close to the bone for you, why not try fish carving? This competitive art sees wooden sculptures of aquatic life judged on their considerable merits.

38 | PARAGLIDING ACCURACY

Winging it

As a concept it is fairly straightforward, if a little terrifying: all you have to do is throw yourself off a mountain and try to land on a target. Fortunately, you have a highly maneuverable paragliding wing strapped to your back.

The sport developed as a cross between paragliding and parachute accuracy. If you're a total paragliding newcomer, you'll find that there are many places where you can try the sport in tandem with an expert to see if you even like the sensation of falling accurately.

Stick the landing

Your target is tiny: an electronic pressure-sensitive pad just 30 cm (12 in.) in diameter. That target will also measure the point of firmest pressure within 0 – 15 cm (0 – 6 in.) of the center, to register a dead-shot bull's-eye. If you miss the pad, your landing will be measured within concentric circles marked out at 0.5 m (1.6 ft), 5 m (16 ft) and 10 m (33 ft) from the center.

Top tip

One of the toughest things about hitting the mark is that you tend to aim your eye for a target, but it's your feet that need to make the hit dead center. Overshooting is one of the first things you will learn to avoid.

Turn into a human dart and throw yourself into sporting history.

On the tee...

Normal golf is tricky. The sand traps can be as deep as a car, the holes can stretch for over 500 m (547 yd.), the wind blows your ball off course and there are full-grown oak trees all over the place. It can take you five hours to get a round in, and leave you seething with frustration.

With mini golf, however, the dangers are much more manageable. All you have to deal with are ramps, plastic pipes and the occasional dwarf windmill. A round takes less than an hour and you're far more likely to hit the clubhouse bar with a smile on your face. Of course, when you get good you'll find that its competitors take it just as seriously as Rory McIlroy and Jordan Spieth take the Masters.

Mainland Europe is the heartland of competitive mini golf. So much so that no player from the UK, U.S., Japan or any outside country has ever reached even the top fifty in the world championships. If you want to make it as a putt-putt champ, you'll need to spend the hours getting to know the European standardized courses and the intricate playing techniques of the game.

The 2015 tournament in Lahti, Finland, drew

Putt your skills on show.

127 players from twenty-one countries and five continents. Players came from as far afield as Kenya and New Zealand to make their maiden appearances at the four-day tournament. Many of the teams arrived several days before the competition to get to know the course and do some practice. The German teams, the defending champions, were the first to arrive in Lahti. This extra preparation paid off, as they became the first country to sweep team and individual gold medals at a single world championships.

Tapping tactics

Unlike a traditional golf putter, a mini-golf putter has rubber on its face. This allows you to impart both topspin and sidespin to the ball to help steer it around gnomes or other obstacles.

Special mini-golf rule

Each player has a maximum of six shots to get the ball in the hole. If you cannot manage this, you score seven points for that hole.

> "It was my life-long dream to host the World Championships on my course and now this dream has become true."
>
> Rolf Bergström, course owner for the 2015 championships

Remember to take your earrings out

A goanna is a large Australian lizard. However, the sport of goanna pulling does not – mercifully – involve any stretching, tugging or yanking of said saurian creatures.

It's actually a test of strength between two human contestants, a bit like a tug of war, but using the back of the head to tug, instead of the hands. You get down on all fours facing your rival, and place your palms on the ground behind a line. A stout leather strap is looped over your heads by the match referee, allowing you to pull backwards against each other. Take the strain against your rival. The referee shouts to start the match and your muscles power into action. Now you simply have to haul your enemy backwards over the win line. This could take seconds or several minutes, depending on how well-matched you are.

It's the lizard-like pose created by the competitors that gives the sport its name – the goanna is a famously ferocious predator, with a thick neck and staring eyes.

You'll need a strong neck and shoulders, tough knees and a crazy stare to win this crown.

Above us only sky

When we say "drones," we don't mean the huge aerial gunships that fly about war zones blowing things up. We're talking about the small and whizzy quadcopter civilian models that are one of the most popular new hobbies out there. Racing them is also very much a thing, and they now have their own world championships.

The 2016 event took place in Hawaii, in the same spectacular valley where Jurassic Park was filmed. There aren't any dinosaurs to snatch these marvellous micro-machines from the sky, but there are still plenty of dangers and pitfalls for the pilots to be wary of, including forests, hills and sheer cliffs.

There are three categories of competition: Speed/Agility, Invitational Freestyle and Team Sport. Each category is made up of several races that run over six action-packed days. In the Extreme Freestyle event you have to pilot your drone in swooping, flipping and spinning moves around natural and man-made obstacles to impress the judges. A popular team event is the Fast Furious Fifty, a NASCAR-style drone race. Your five-strong team of pilot, co-pilot and three pit crew have to do whatever it takes to get your drone around fifty laps of the aerial circuit. If you crash or hit the safety netting you have to recover your airframe quickly, do some hot running repairs and take to the air once more. This is a big, fast, frantic and very, very loud race.

Zoom your way into the final

The best way to guarantee a place at the world championships is to qualify in an officially sanctioned event in your home country. You can also enter the last pre-qualifying race held a couple of days before the main event, to gain one of the ten wildcard spots.

As close to being in a *Star Wars* battle scene as you're likely to get.

111

42 | CHEESE ROLLING

How to get in a pickle

Cheese isn't normally known for its athletic ability. It usually just sits there, perhaps oozing a bit, and you can easily get yourself a piece by going after it with a knife and a cracker. At Cooper's Hill, however, several cheeses are rolled down a hill every year, and to catch them – and be crowned World Cheese Rolling Champion – you'll need to be fleet of foot, tough of body, and a little bit crazy in the head.

What happens if you gather so much momentum that you can't stop? Don't worry, at the bottom are several strong-armed and fast-on-their-feet members of Brockworth Rugby Club – the "Catchers." They're there to safely hold onto any careening competitors.

Ideal if you can
move your legs like a
windmill and have a
good head for heights.

A risky roll

The event is the stuff of a Health & Safety official's
nightmare. The hill is steep – VERY steep. Contestants
start off trying to run down the hill, but this soon turns
into a cartwheeling tumble. Once your balance has
gone, your only goal is damage limitation. Keep your
face away from other runners' flying feet and try not
to break your ankles.

There are always a few injuries, and the highest
toll was in 1997, when thirty-three people needed
medical attention. Spectators also occasionally take
a tumble, and sometimes a wayward cheese has
been known to roll into the crowd.

113

Ready to roll

The action starts at noon on the late May bank holiday. The MC organizes events, and for each race he will give the following commands:

"**ONE** to be ready!"
"**TWO** to be steady!"
"**THREE** to prepare!"

At this point the guest "roller" releases the cheese, which sets off down the hill at an ever-more terrifying speed. The MC continues:

"and **FOUR** to be off!"

And the competitors chuck themselves down the slope in pursuit.

The first person to reach the foot of the hill wins the cheese, while second and third places receive a

---

Did you know? During the Second World War, food rationing meant that a wooden "cheese" was chased. Real cheeses were reintroduced in 1954, after rationing ended.

small cash prize. As for the idea of actually catching the cheese – forget it. The flighty foodstuff has a one-second head start and can easily top 112 km/h (70 mph). There are five downhill races, including one for ladies. There are also four races where competitors simply have to run up the hill, not chasing anything but their own breath.

Double Gloucester cheeses are traditionally made in a wheel shape, and a racing cheese weighs around 3.6 kg (8 lb). Since 1988, all racing cheeses have been hand-made by Diana Smart of Churcham, Gloucestershire, using milk from her herd of Brown Swiss, Holstein and Gloucester cows. She is the only person in Gloucestershire still making Double Gloucester cheeses by hand in the traditional way.

You have to be at least 18 years old to take part in the downhill races. As for training and technique, Chris Anderson, who has won fifteen cheeses over eleven years, uses a combination of very fast foot movements and stuntman-style body rolls when he goes to ground.

They're all barking mad

The Lumberjack World Championships is the granddaddy of all woodland challenges. It has twenty-one spectacular competitions including several chopping and sawing events and some other special challenges, like log-rolling, boom run and pole climb, described here.

Log-rolling

You and your competitor – or "birlers" as you are known – step off a dock onto a floating log. Now, simply standing on this giant floating stick is hard, and at this point you are allowed to grab hold of a pole held by an attendant to keep your balance. When you are both steady and balanced, the referee will start the match with the command, "Throw your poles." You are now both loose on the log and you have to "birl," or spin it, with your special caulked birling shoes, and throw your adversaries off balance and into the water. If you give your opponent a "wetting," you go through to the next round. The golden rule of log-rolling is "never take your eyes off your opponent's feet."

Boom run

You have to race in a head-to-head contest against a rival across a chain of floating logs. The two of you line up on the dock, facing a line of "booms" – floating logs linked together end-to-end. At the command "Go" you dash across the chain to the far dock, go around a marker and run back across the pond on the boom logs. If you start before the word "Go" you get a ten-second penalty. Your key skill is to keep up a good pace – like riding a bicycle, boom running is easier to do when you have some momentum.

Pole climb

You have to scale a 27.4 m (90 ft) cedar pole and get back down to the ground as fast as you can. Pairs of competitors race each other on adjacent poles. You must touch the pole every 4.5 m (15 ft) on the way down – so no one is tempted to do their best flying-squirrel impression. Your only aids are traditional climbing spurs and steel-core climbing ropes.

Beavers are not allowed to enter.

117

"People just like to have fun and the spectators come because they like to see people get wet and they like to see people sink. It's two hours of family fun and slapstick entertainment involving household tin baths that your granny will have used in front of the fire."

Organizer, David Collister

The one event that's sure to float your boat.

World sport meets personal hygiene

Bathtubs are designed to hold water in, not keep it out. But that didn't stop the Castletown Ale Drinkers' Society from starting the crazy World Tin Bath Championships (mind you, there's not much that can stop the Castletown Ale Drinkers' Society).

The event takes place every July in the inviting waters of Castletown harbor. It draws hundreds of spectators and raises a lot of money for local charities.

Ready to make a splash

Competitors decorate their bathtubs and don a silly costume. Whether this helps in any way with the craft's overall seaworthiness is a point that is up for debate. They then have to take to the waters of the harbor and gather at the starting line. When the gun goes off it's a fast and frantic paddle to the far end of the 400-m (437-yd) course. The winner is meant to be the first to cross the finish line. However, the baths are not known for their hydrodynamic stability, and if everyone sinks then the person who paddled the furthest before going under is the champ.

If you want to launch a world championship bid, it'll pay to practice some paddling. Despite the silly costumes, competition is stiff – there are usually around 100 competitors from the British Isles, Europe and the United States.

Top tin tip

Tie some floats, such as old plastic bottles onto your bathtub. That way, if it does sink, you won't lose it forever to Davy Jones' Locker, and your grandma can still have her regular soap-down.

119

A tale of two spitters

This sport has been tried, to some extent, by anyone who has ever eaten a cherry. But it was refined into a competitive activity by Herb Teichman, an American cherry farmer.

For some reason it enjoyed a blaze of popularity in Switzerland in the mid-1980s and spread to Britain, Germany, Australia, Canada, China, Mexico, Ireland, Poland and Russia. Usually such an international rush of enthusiasm would be an entirely welcome thing. However, a serious controversy flared up that nearly tore the cherry-pit-spitting world apart.

Trouble began when Lucien Mosimann, the president of the Swiss Cherry-Pit Spitting Association, announced that Thomas Steinhauer, a fellow Swiss, had broken the world record set by an American rival. Steinhauer shot a pit 25.2 m (82.7 ft), trouncing the 22.5 m (74 ft) record held by American champion Rick "Pellet Gun" Krause.

Krause couldn't believe his record had been so thoroughly beaten and when he checked the Swiss figures, he noticed a discrepancy. It turned out Steinhauer had achieved his feat using Swiss rules of spitting, which over the years had changed from the American way of doing things.

Antisocial behavior turned into an accuracy competition.

Spitting Swiss-style: You can take two steps before spitting. Your spit is measured to the point where the stone hits the ground.

Spitting American-style: You spit from the spot. Your spit is measured to the point the stone rolls to.

Debate raged over which was the official standard, and even the Guinness Book of Records was perplexed. To settle the matter, the sport has turned to academics at Michigan State University to develop universal standards for an upcoming "spit-off" that will unify the international titles. If you want to take part in the unification championship, these are the conditions you will need to master.

The regulations state that only a Montmorency variety of cherry is to be used. It should be presented at a temperature of 13°C (55°F). Contestants take up position behind a foul line on a 1.22 m by 2.44 m (4 ft by 8 ft) platform, at the end of a 6.1 m by 30.5 m (20 ft by 100 ft) spitting court. Official events must have distance judges, line judges, a timekeeper, scorekeeper, pit sweeper, and a handicap-measurement judge. You then have to pick your cherry, pop it into your mouth, and you'll have 60 seconds to gobble the fruit, clean the pit and fire it down the court – and yourself into history.

46 | COMBAT JUGGLING

"To begin, all you do is try not to drop. Then you try not to be the first person out. Then you try to do a single successful attack. Then you learn to move and duck and dodge. Then you learn to win!"

Combat juggling no.1, Luke Burrage

Juggling is hard enough without someone trying to knock your clubs away.

Join the club

Combat juggling is a sport where two or more players juggling three clubs go into battle to try and make their opponent drop their clubs. Combat can be played individually against a single opponent (one-on-one-combat), between teams of two or more players each, or in a group where everyone plays against everyone else.

Competitors are called to the stage. They stand a few paces apart and face each other. At the referee's command they start juggling their three clubs in front of their chests, trying to get into a confident, smooth rhythm. Slowly, they edge towards each other, throwing feints, stamping a foot or calling to try to put their opponent off. When they're within striking distance, they look for an opportunity and then pounce.

The basic attacking move is to throw one of your clubs high in the air to buy yourself a little time, then dart into your opponent's personal space and try and knock one of their clubs out of reach. You then have to catch sight of your own club and collect it again. As a spectator, the sport appears as a sort of soothing, gently coordinated dance interspersed with sudden moments of extreme violence.

Rules

You can only attack your opponents' clubs, not their bodies or heads. Anyone who is no longer juggling at least three clubs (because they dropped, collected, or had a club stolen by an opponent) is out of the game or loses a point.

Group combat: In the sport's most common form, several players compete in an open group combat. They each attempt to interfere with other players' juggling, with the winner being the last to remain juggling three clubs.

One-on-one-combat: The player who doesn't drop their club gains a point in each round. The competitor with the highest total becomes the winner. Often there are several rounds.

The de facto world championship competition is the fight night at the annual European Juggling Convention, the sport's largest gathering.

Sole champion

A nurse works her way through the nervous competitors, checking they are fit and can be cleared for action. And that they don't have a nasty fungal infection or scraggly toenails. That done, the first two competitors form a pair of opposing feet on the championship podiatric podium. They lock big toes, and on the word from the referee, attempt to wrestle their opponent to the edge of the playing area.

Toe wrestling is very similar to arm wrestling, but played with a different appendage. Contestants lock their big toes for the best of three bouts: right foot first, then left, then right again to finish.

The sport was first played in 1974 by four friends drinking at the Ye Olde Royal Oak Inn in Wetton, Staffordshire. Their inspiration was simple: they were so irritated by England's recent sporting performances that they wanted to create a sport that an English athlete might actually stand a chance of triumphing in. Their reasoning was that if they quietly created a new sport that no one else knew about, the country would be able to finally claim a world champion. After trying out the competitive possibilities of "ear wrestling" and "push of war" (with a scaffolding pole), they decided on toe wrestling, and local Mick Dawson was duly crowned champ. He retained his title the next year, but in 1976 he was beaten by a visiting Canadian.

Training tips

An elastic loop for stretching between your toes is the ideal piece of training kit. You could also work on your thigh and calf strength and knee flexibility.

Dirty tactics

Some players when they know they are going to lose will employ the technique of "flicking off." It can be hard for the referee to tell whether the loss of grip was accidental or intentional.

"Toe wrestling is the one sport England always wins at. We get hammered at everything else."

World champion, Alan "Nasty" Nash

Are you ready to toe the line?

125

My, what sharp teeth you have

"Sharks of the land," "piranhas with feet" and "furry evil" are just some of the affectionate terms that handlers use instead of *mustela putorius*, the official name of the domesticated ferret. Ferrets were bred for their unsurpassed ability to run into a rabbit warren and massacre every last inhabitant in a matter of minutes. Lightning fast, with razor-sharp claws and teeth like needles, ferrets are furry, four-legged killing machines.

Many vets refuse to treat these fearsome little beasts, and you might think that even keeping a ferret would be dangerous enough. But many sportsmen in the north of England enjoy testing each other's mettle in a competition where you have to put a live ferret down your pants and see how long you can keep it there. This is ferret-legging.

Why? Please tell us why

Practitioners say that ferret-legging (also called "put 'em down") started centuries ago, at a the time when only the rich were allowed to keep animals used for hunting. This forced poachers to stash their illicit ferrets in their pants. The sport enjoyed a resurgence among Yorkshire coal miners (a notoriously hardy breed themselves) in the 1970s, and there are still regular competitions held there. If you want to be crowned world champ, that's where you'll need to strut your ferretty stuff.

It's a simple, if seriously dangerous, sport to engage in. You just tie your pants at the ankles and drop one of the pocket-sized carnivores into them. Pull your belt tight to stop the spirited little fellow from leaping straight back out again, and then wait until you can take no more of the pain. The winner is the last one to release the animal. The world record stands at an incredible 5 hours and 30 minutes.

It makes other extreme sports look tame.

Ferret facts

Adult ferrets measure roughly 46 cm (18 in.) from nose to tail.

Ferret-legging competitors cannot be drunk or drugged, nor can the ferrets be sedated.

You must allow the ferrets free access from one leg to the other, and the ferrets must have a full set of teeth that must not have been filed or otherwise blunted.

There was once an attempt to introduce a version of the sport aimed at ladies – "ferret-busting" – in which female contestants popped ferrets down their blouses. For some reason this didn't catch on.

you have much to learn about mushing

Doggone it

It's hard not to fall in love with a sport in which the contestants are all having a fantastic time. And one look at a team of sled dogs will tell you that these winter woofers just love it. Their drivers seem to have a pretty good time too…

Sled dog racing declined in popularity once snowmobiles were invented, but as these machines don't lick your face and keep you warm at night, more and more winter racers are returning to "mushing."

There are three basic types of sled dog race:

Sprints – These are short races of around 6.5 – 40 km (4 – 25 miles). Sprints are usually two- or three-day events where heats are run on successive days, with the same dogs on the same course.

Mid-distance – These races cover distances of 160 – 480 km (100 – 300 miles) and are either heat

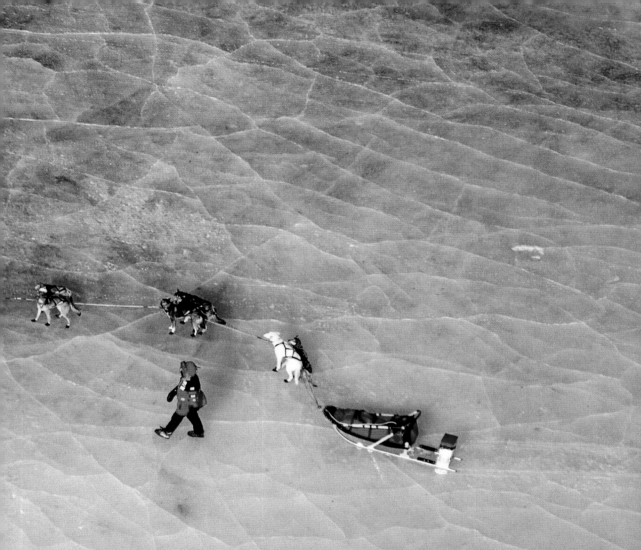

races of 22 – 130 km (14 – 80 miles) per day, or continuous races of 160 – 320 km (100 – 200 miles).

Long-distance – These can range from 480 km (300 miles) to more than 1,600 km (1,000 miles). The famous Iditarod race in Alaska is run over 1,688 km (1,049 miles) by a team of twenty-one dogs and takes 9 – 15 days.

The official world championship is the "Fur Rondy" (or "Fur Rendezvous"), held in Anchorage, Alaska, every February. This festival grew out of the swap meets attended by local fur trappers. The championship race itself is a three-day, 120-km (75-mile) event.

Tips for training

Snow is usually essential for this sport, so you should live in, or relocate to, a cold country. However, if that isn't practicable, you can put wheels on your sled, call it a cart, and head off into the woods.

It's sand-sational

There aren't many sports with as low a barrier to entry as sand sculpting. Most of us built our first sand castle while we were still in diapers and put half the sand we could get hold of in our mouths. However, at the world championship-level of sand sculpting, it is a very different thing.

Sand castles become sand skyscrapers. Basic moats are turned into cascading rivers. A simple face is now the Mona Lisa rendered in three dimensions. They can also take on gargantuan proportions. The largest sand castle made in a contest by a single person was 5.5 m (18 ft) tall and used a ton of sand. The world's tallest team sand castle was 15.1 m (49.55 ft) high, took ten days to construct and used 300 truckloads of sand.

The world championship was first held in Harrison Hot Springs in Harrison, British Columbia, Canada – the fame of the competition earned it the nickname "Harrisand." The contest is structured with solo, double and team categories, and you have a set amount of time to create your world-beating, beach-based masterpiece.

Top tip

One of the hardest skills you must learn is keeping the sand moist enough. Too dry and the fine grains won't stick together; too wet and your sculpture could slump into a soggy mess.

Tools

Many competitors only use their hands, but shovels, buckets and carving tools are allowed. You can also use forms of wood or plastic to give strength to taller constructions. Apart from that, it's just sand, water and your imagination.

Can you create a masterpiece before wind and tide do their worst?

MASTER SAND SCULPTOR

Justin Gordon

Friends, Romans, countrymen...

Every year, ten contestants from all over the world deliver a seven-minute speech in front of a packed auditorium to be judged by a panel of highly experienced public speakers. The prize is the honor of being the world-champion public speaker. Plus, you get a large, angular glass trophy. If the thought of getting up and speaking in such an exposed public place chills you to the bone – don't despair! You are the very person who the organizers of the championships would love to get involved.

Your steps to the world stage

The official world championships are run by Toastmasters International, a not-for-profit organization that promotes the benefits of better public speaking. You can pop into one of their 15,400 clubs in 135 countries and simply start with a single speech. As you learn and get better at telling stories, you'll progress through area, district and semi-final competitions before earning your place in the International Speech Contest. Even if you don't make it to the elite level, it's one of those activities that is bound to have unexpected benefits in your professional and social life. It may even be the start of a whole new career.

Stand up and stand out.

This was impossible...and yet here it is... If I can do this, think about the thing you thought you could never do. And remember you can do it too.

Mohammed Qahtani, Saudi Arabia, World Public Speaking Champion 2015 on what winning meant to him

52 | PEASHOOTING

WHERE CAMBRIDGESHIRE, ENGLAND | **SINCE** 1971
USEFUL EQUIPMENT PEA, PEASHOOTER, YOUR BREATH

Blow the competition away

The World Peashooting Championship has been held every year since 1971 in the village of Witcham near Ely. The Open Championship is unrestricted to all genders, ages and nationalities. As long as you can puff, you can play. There are also separate competitions for Ladies, Children at Primary School and Teams.

History of the Peashoot

The event was started by the village schoolmaster, Mr. Tyson, who caught some boisterous pupils pinging their unfortunate schoolmates with peas and at first confiscated the offending weapons. Perhaps Mr. Tyson remembered how much fun he had had doing the same thing when he was a boy, because rather than punish the children further, he decided to hold a World Peashooting Championship. It was also the perfect way to raise much-needed funds for the village hall.

135

You can bring your own peashooter or buy one on the day from the White Horse Pub, where there is a practice area. And refreshments, obviously.

Peashooters must not be shared by contestants. The peashooter may be made of any material but must not exceed 30 cm (12 in.) in length and may include sighting devices. Note: laser pointers or similar laser-assisted peashooters are not allowed in the children's competition.

Peas must be fired by blowing with the mouth. The distance from the target will be 3.66 m (12 ft). In the children's competition it will be 3 m (10 ft) for those aged 8 and over, and 2.4 m (8 ft) for those aged 7 and under.

The target is formed from three circles of putty: the inner circle scores five points, the middle circle three and the outer circles one point. You have to shoot five peas at a target and must use the peas (maple peas) provided by officials.

The highest sixteen scores in the open championship the highest eight scores in the ladies' and the children's competition) will qualify for the knock-out round.

Contestants' names are drawn to decide their opponents and the order of play. Each pair of contestants face off by shooting five peas alternately. The winner of each match will qualify for the semi-final. In the event of a tie, the match will be decided by "sudden death."

For the team championship, teams must have four named players and the four top-scoring teams will qualify for the second round.

In the semi-final stage, the contestants shoot ten peas alternately. The winners progress to the final to shoot for the championship trophy and worldwide fame.

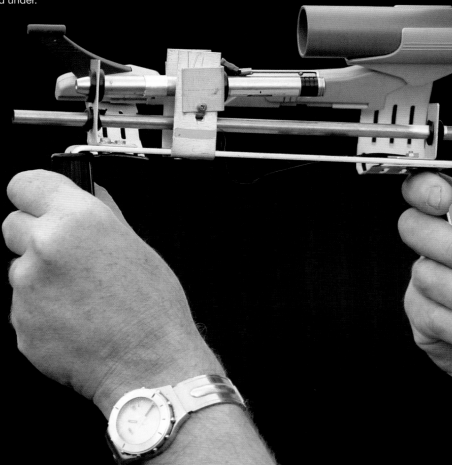

shooting

Take aim for **glory**.

53 | DOG DANCING

Barking mad

Perhaps your dog can do a trick or two. But could it do three minutes' worth of tricks, in a row, on demand and in time to a piece of music? More importantly, can you do the same? Because "dog dancing" really only tells half the story – the event is about dogs and their owners dancing together in a beautifully choreographed routine.

Costumes, creativity and partnership are what you must pay particular attention to if you want to excel in what is also known as "musical canine freestyle." Basic moves you can try include leg weaving, sending the dog away and moving together at a distance. Once the two of you get used to dancing together, you can progress to more dramatic tricks such as jumping, spinning, bowing, rolling over and dancing on the spot. For your big finish, you can work on an explosive move where your dog jumps into your arms or up and over your back.

Training

You should start by getting your pooch used to doing obedience tricks on both sides of your body, not just the left side as in standard obedience heeling. When creating your routine, start with two or three moves linked together and build these up by joining them into sequences.

Top tip

No matter how innovative you and your dog's routine is, if it doesn't follow the rhythm, you won't score well. Keep those paws moving to the beat...

Is your pet woofer a hot hoofer?

Keepie-uppie times a thousand

What if you're skillful at soccer but don't have many friends? It doesn't mean you have to miss out on your chance of sporting glory. You can simply take up freestyle soccer and do away with the need for team-mates. It's all about doing as many cool tricks as you can, and thankfully no one is trying to kick the ball away from you while you're doing so.

Players have been showing off their solo soccer skills for as long as the game has been around, but the team game has always grabbed the headlines. Diego Maradona was one of the first professional soccer players to showcase his freestyle skills, and in the 1990s some freestyle artists started to draw more attention. In the 2000s, thanks to Brazilian soccer icon Ronaldinho starring in a series of Nike commercials, the sport exploded in popularity. The first official world freestyle championship was held in Kuala Lumpur in 2011.

For once the goal is not to score a goal.

WHERE WORLDWIDE | **SINCE** 2011

USEFUL EQUIPMENT BALL, FEET

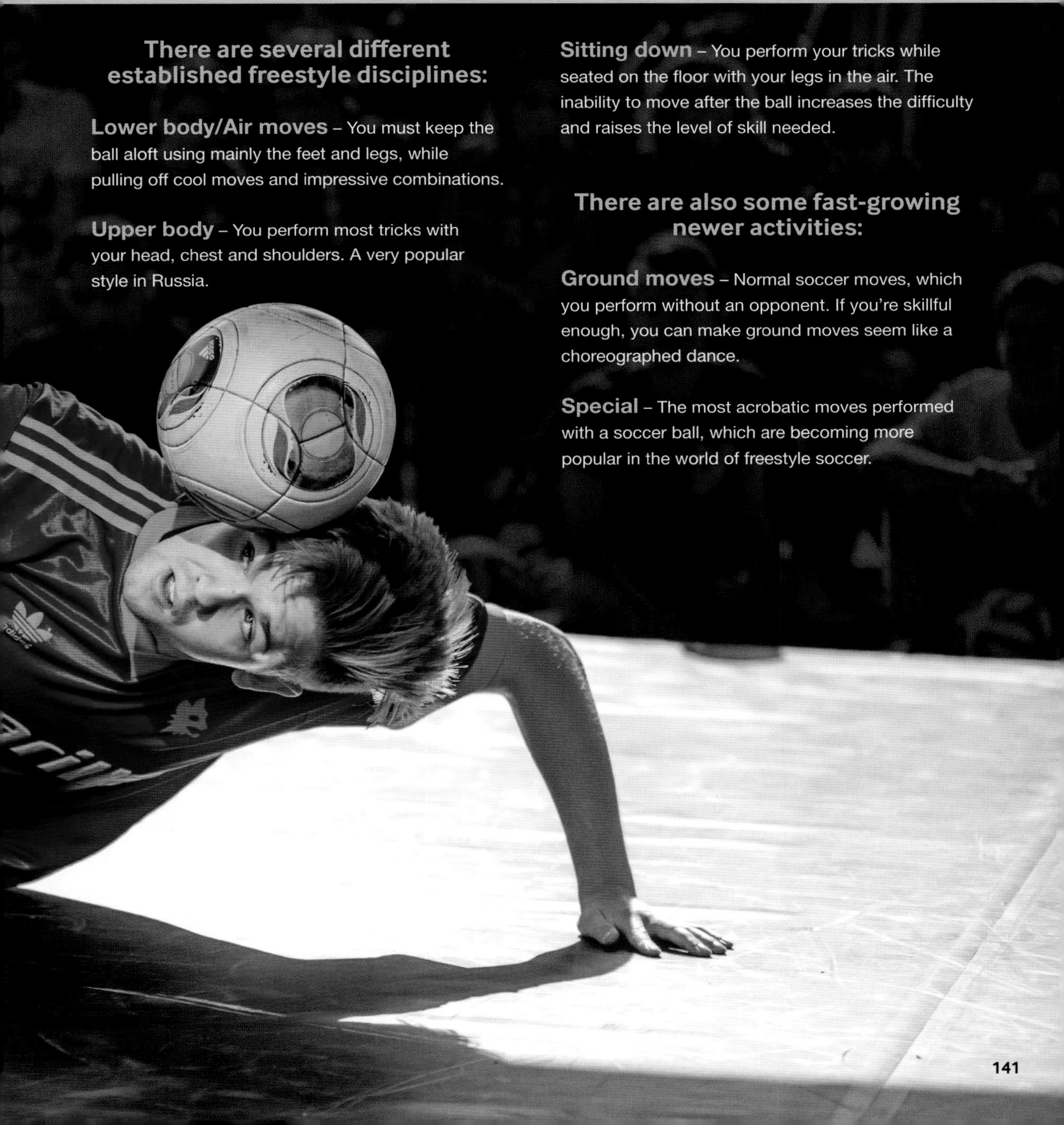

There are several different established freestyle disciplines:

Lower body/Air moves – You must keep the ball aloft using mainly the feet and legs, while pulling off cool moves and impressive combinations.

Upper body – You perform most tricks with your head, chest and shoulders. A very popular style in Russia.

Sitting down – You perform your tricks while seated on the floor with your legs in the air. The inability to move after the ball increases the difficulty and raises the level of skill needed.

There are also some fast-growing newer activities:

Ground moves – Normal soccer moves, which you perform without an opponent. If you're skillful enough, you can make ground moves seem like a choreographed dance.

Special – The most acrobatic moves performed with a soccer ball, which are becoming more popular in the world of freestyle soccer.

Just be careful you don't get breathless with excitement.

Go on, take the plunge

Octopush, or underwater hockey as it's also known, was invented in Southsea, England, in 1954 by scuba divers who wanted something less chilly to do over the winter.

Rules of play

Six players from each side line up at opposite ends of a pool (each team also has four rolling substitutes) and the puck is dropped into the middle. A gong gets things going and the players take a breath and dive under to get the puck. Their aim is simply to shove the puck into their opponent's goal. Players wear a diving mask, snorkel and fins, and carry a short stick for playing the puck.

Each match has two halves of 10 – 15 minutes, although this rises to 20 minutes for the world championships. This international contest has been held every two years since 1980, moving from country to country.

Improve your pool prowess

If you want to get to the top in the depths, you'll need to be a strong swimmer with a knack for holding your breath. You'll need good hand-to-goggled-eye coordination.

Don't expect worldwide fame

Although octopush is a physical, skillful and fun activity, it isn't the most thrilling of spectator sports. Most of the action occurs deep below the surface with the players occasionally bobbing up to grab a breath.

An ancient art

The game of marbles is older than recorded history – archaeologists have found the miniature spheres in ancient Egyptian and Roman tombs. It has been popular in school playgrounds and English pub gardens for centuries and the official world championship has been regularly held outside the Greyhound pub in Tinsley Green, England, since 1932. But local history maintains that the tournament is much older than that.

Why Tinsley Green?

Legend tells the tale of a contest from the reign of Elizabeth I, when two young suitors, Giles and Hodge, battled for the hand of a Tinsley Green milk maiden named Joan. The two young gentlemen faced off in the most popular sports of the day in a week-long contest. Hodge triumphed at several fighting challenges: singlestick, backsword, quarter staff, cudgel play, wrestling and cock throwing. Giles won at the games demanding accuracy: archery, cricket-a-wicket, tilting at quintain, Turk's head, stoolball and tipcat. With the score tied at 6-6, Joan herself chose marbles as the deciding game. On Good Friday in the year 1588, Giles knocked Hodge's marbles clear from the circle and claimed his fair prize.

The Marbles World Championship is open to players of all ages and nationalities, and in recent

It's time to knuckle down and play this championship for keeps.

years teams from Australia, Belgium, Canada, Estonia, Ireland, France, Germany, Japan, Netherlands, Wales and the U.S. have all challenged the home English teams. There are several different games that you can play with marbles, but for the official world championships you'll need to start practicing the discipline known as "Ring Taw." In the U.S., this is often called "Ringer" and in Germany it's known as "Englisches Ringspiel."

The arena is a raised concrete ring 1.8 m (6 ft) in diameter, covered with sand. Forty-nine target marbles are grouped closely together in the center. These marbles are around 12 mm (0.5 in.) in diameter. Two teams of six players then take turns trying to smash the marbles out of the ring by pinging them with a "shooter" marble, also known as a "taw" or "tolley." The taw is larger, around 18 mm in diameter (0.75 in.).

When shooting your taw you must touch your knuckle against the ground – this is where the phrase "to knuckle down" comes from. (The phrase "playing for keeps" also has its origins in the sport – in such a game, whoever wins keeps all the marbles.) The first team to knock twenty-five marbles out of the ring is the winner.

Fair not foul

You can't shift your taw closer to the target marbles – this is known as "cabbaging." Nor can you move your shooting hand in an advantageous way – that's a foul known as "fudging." Should your clothing touch a marble while it is in motion, you will be penalized for "blocking." If you commit a foul, you get no score for that shot and your turn ends. If you make three foul shots in a game, you will be disqualified.

Fascinating marble facts

Women were banned from the main tournament in 1970 because too many of them were wearing miniskirts.

Originally, marbles were made of clay.

The official tournament switched to glass in 1962.

Comedy movie legends Laurel and Hardy tried their hands at becoming world marbles champions in 1947.

It's time to
get a slice of
the action.

All rise for the champ

If anyone has ever complimented your homemade chocolate cake, you could perhaps try your icing hand in the world cake championships. But if your spongecake occasionally has a soggy bottom, you'd better start practicing – the standards, like the cakes, can be incredibly high.

The world championship, which takes place in Milan, Italy, is organized every two years by the deliciously named International Federation of Pastry, Ice Cream and Chocolate. Each championship has a theme, to give your creative skills a spark of inspiration. For example, the theme for 2017 is "Discovering the World of Chocolate and Coffee." A wonderful world to discover, we can all agree on that.

There are also international-standard competitions in the U.S., UK, Australia and many other countries – prove yourself in one of these challenges and you could have what it takes to triumph in the "worlds."

Cake decorating is a team event; each team must have one coach and one competitor. The contest lasts for an arduous eight hours, starting at 7 am and finishing for final presentation at 3 pm.

Cake Categories

There are three categories of cake making, and you must excel in all of them:

Public Exhibition – Your cake must be brought already finished and decorated, although you may choose to mount it on the day. The base should be a maximum diameter of 80 cm (31 in.), but the height is at your discretion. There must be more than one layer, and all supports should be covered with something edible such as sugar paste, chocolate, almond paste or marzipan.

Taste Test – Here you have to produce three cakes 18 cm (7 in.) in diameter that are the same shape and flavor. A jury of cake experts will judge you not only on deliciousness and texture, but the consistency of those qualities over the three cakes. The cake for the taste test must be decorated with the same material used in the "Public Exhibition" cake and in the cake for the "Live Decorating." All teams must bring their own specialist equipment such as sugar lamps, knives and spatulas. You should bake your bases (sponge, shortbread, biscuit, meringue, etc.) before the competition; but you must create and assemble all the internal fillings (cream, buttercream, etc.) in the heat of the competition.

Live Decorating – In this challenging category you must reproduce and decorate your "Public Exhibition" cake live, in front of the crowd and judges. Any elements that need a long time to dry (e.g. pastillage, gum paste, icing) can be brought along ready-prepared, but must be assembled as a live demonstration during the competition.

Judging

Your score will be composed as follows:

50 percent – Artistic Impression of the cake for "Public exhibition" and the cake for "Decorated live exhibition." This includes adherence to the theme, difficulty in performance, the techniques used and innovation (which could involve royal icing, painting, modelling, isomalt, caramel sugar, sugar crumb, gum paste, various types of pastillage, airbrushing and 3D effects).

30 percent – Taste Test. This includes combined tastes, different cake structures, difficulty in performance, cake innovation.

20 percent – General Impression. This includes cleanliness during the work, order in the workstation, organization of the work, brochure and recipe book, and final presentation of the table.

Should you triumph, your prize is a gold medal, a "Certificate of Honor" and €2,500. You will also have plenty to eat on the way home.

58 | HANDWRITING | Do you have the craft to be world champ-pen?

WHERE NEW YORK, U.S. | **SINCE** 1991 | **USEFUL EQUIPMENT** PEN, PAPER

You've got to hand it to these champs

In our days of typing and tapping, beautiful penmanship is a fast-fading art. Even legible handwriting can be rare. So with the motto "Every human has the right to write well," the World Handwriting Championship is a contest to be embraced; an elegant remnant of a slower, more thoughtful time. There are five age groups:

- Under 8
- Pre-teens (8 – 12)
- Teens (13 – 19)
- Adults (20 – 65)
- Seniors (over 65)

However, the overall world champ-pen (yes, that is how they are officially known) can come from any age group. There were 606 entries in the 2014 competition, and the overall winner was a 12-year-old girl from Nepal, called Swarima Shakya. Her flawless and exquisite script simply stunned the panel.

Within each group, the judges will assess the writing within two main categories:

Functional handwriting – This is script that strives for legibility, speed and fluency without artistic effects. There are two sub-categories: Cursive, where 50 percent or more of the letters are joined; and Manuscript (print-writing), where fewer than half of the letters are linked.

Artistic handwriting – In this category, you can use a monoline or calligraphy marker, pen or brush along with decorative strokes, flourishes, or combinations of shading and hairlines to create an artistic effect.

Entry to the championship is simple – all you have to do is write out the following sage quotation in your own hand:

HANDWRITING: that action of emotion, of thought, and of decision that has recorded the history of mankind, revealed the genius of invention, and disclosed the inmost depths of the heart. Handwriting ties us to the thoughts and deeds of our forebears and serves as an irrevocable link to our humanity. No machine or technology can replace the contribution or continuing importance of this skill. It has been necessary in every age and is just as vital to civilization as our next breath.

Michael R. Sull

Then just send your handwriting sample to the New York offices of the championship to be judged. The expert judges will consider it against several exacting criteria: choice of layout and margin; consistency of letter size, neatness, spacing between letters and words, general appearance and finally spelling.

Hop to it

Rabbits love to hop, everyone knows that. But you may not be aware that they also really rather like jumping. Kaninhop, the Swedish sport of bunny jumping, has turned the creatures' natural leaping ability into an unlikely, yet very endearing, competitive sport.

The basic sport is very similar to showjumping: rabbits have to jump over a series of obstacles in the fastest time possible, with as few strikes as possible. Building on that basic concept, there are several different jumping disciplines.

 Straight path – The jumps are located on a straight line.

 Crooked path – The rabbit will have to make turns and take the obstacles in a certain order.

 Long jump – The rabbit gets three attempts at each distance. The world record is 3 m (9.8 ft).

 High jump – The rabbit gets three attempts at each height. The world record is 99.5 cm (39 in.).

 Points jumping – Ten obstacles are placed in a circle. The rabbit has one minute to jump over as many as it can. It earns a point for every passed obstacle and the bunny with the most points wins.

Like showjumping, but with rabbits instead of horses.

 Dual jumping – Two parallel paths set up with identical obstacles, with two rabbits jumping simultaneously.

 Slalom jumping – Barriers are set up side by side, so that the rabbit has to jump on a slalom path.

 Cross-country classes – Barriers are set up on hilly land. Obstacles are of different heights. Often, a mountain path is much longer than in normal jumping.

"You slowly work with them to go over the jumps by placing your hand under the front legs and the other hand under the bottom and actually placing them over the low bars. They eventually catch on to what you would like them to do."

Linda Hoover, president of the Rabbit Hopping Organization of America (on training novice rabbits)

Your rabbit must be at least 4 months old to race, and at least 8 months old to compete in the high jump or long jump. Rabbits over 5 years old can compete in the Veteran class.

Lapine leaping has now spread far from its Scandinavian homeland, with many clubs and competitions in Europe, the U.S., Canada and Japan. But Sweden is still the place to go if you want (your rabbit) to be world champion. So high is the standard that the national championship there is the de facto world title.

Top tips

It's vital that you have a leash for your rabbit. The creatures may suddenly get the urge, as rabbits do, to run off and make friends with an attractive bunny on the far side of the arena. Such activity is frowned upon in competitive kaninhop.

When choosing your rabbit, avoid large and heavy breeds, and Angoras. Rabbits with thick coats tend to get hot quickly and will stop hopping when they are overheated.

Let the games begin

The annual World Boardgaming Championships draws around 2,000 international competitors, all aiming to be crowned champion of games that you can spill your coffee on.

Every year, 100 games are selected to be played in the championships. Every event of this "century group" is ranked from two to six; this is the number of places that will win a plaque, or "wood" in the vernacular of the competition.

Although many competitors are highly experienced, you do not need to be an expert player to try your hand at glory. Many gaming events are designed for beginners or are coached for first-time players (the game is taught during or just prior to events).

The championships have a strict focus on the competitive play of boardgames, and do not include computer games, miniatures, role-playing or collectible card games. Popular games include

Roll the dice and take your chance.

Diplomacy, Kingmaker, History of the World, Risk, Slapshot and Panzergruppe Guderian.

Taking winning seriously

If you "get wood" you will take away a 20-cm (8-in.) shield plaque (all other plaques are rectangular), a "Centurion" t-shirt and bragging rights. The organizers do not offer cash prizes, as they have discovered that even small monetary rewards tend to bring out the worst in some people.

"The public is often unduly intimidated by competition. The fact of the matter is that no one ever bettered themselves in any endeavor without getting beat along the way. The best teacher is observing the tactics of more experienced players first hand. So what if you lose? You'll come out of the event a wiser player than you entered it. Today's loser is tomorrow's champion in the making."

World Boardgaming
Championships website

155

Par for the course

Disc golf is a delightfully simple game – take a Frisbee, throw it at a series of targets, get to the end in as few throws as possible. If you've ever thrown a Frisbee around a park, you'll soon get the hang of disc golf (or "frolf" as it's also delightfully called). However, the game's straightforward concept has developed into a varied, challenging and increasingly popular sport. If you want to be the champ, you'd better learn the finer points of frolf.

Guide to the game

Rather than putt into a hole, you must hit a basket with hanging chains that check the disc's flight. Other than that, the game is very similar to golf. Just as you use different clubs at different points on a golf hole, so too do you use different discs on a frolf hole.

Putters are usually standard throwing discs, such as the Frisbee. They will fly slowly but straight and are used when you get close to the basket.

Mid-range discs are what beginners often learn the sport with. They have slightly sharper edges than a putter to help them cut through the air better and give greater range.

Drivers are usually recognized by their sharp, bevelled edge and have most of their mass concentrated on the outer rim of the disc rather than distributed equally throughout.

Disc golf was invented in the United States, and the country has 4,000 of the world's 5,000 disc golf courses. The annual world championship moves from state to state and there are many other professional and amateur tournaments.

Bag a birdie and you could soar like an eagle.

Top techniques

Top golfers use spin to fade and draw the ball, and disc golfers have a wide variety of techniques to control their shot. If you're right-handed, a standard backhand throw will tend to make the disc fall to the left. A forehand throw will make it fall to the right. These directions are reversed for left-handed throwers. As well as the standard backhand and forehand, there are several specialist throwing styles:

 The Tomahawk – Hold your Frisbee perpendicular to the ground and throw it with an overhand motion.

 The Roller – Rather than fly up the fairway, this throw will send the disc rolling along the ground. A useful throw when the ground is even.

 The Thumber – An overhand throw with your thumb placed under the disc.

 The Turbo-Putt – You hold a putter disc with your thumb in the middle underneath and your fingers curling around the rim. Now throw the Frisbee like a dart. The Turbo-Putt is very accurate over short distances.

WHERE NORTHAMPTONSHIRE, ENGLAND | **SINCE** 1965
ESSENTIAL EQUIPMENT KNUCKLE PROTECTORS

Your hopes dangle by a thread

In the game of conkers, brave duellists string up nuts of the horse chestnut tree (*Aesculus hippocastanum*) and do knuckle-bashing battle with them. It has been a favorite autumn pastime of British schoolchildren for centuries, but it evolved from a much older game called "conquerors," which was originally played with snail or other shells ("concha" is Latin for shellfish, or shell).

The world championships have been held every October (the best month for conkers) in the ancient English market town of Oundle. Ashton Conker Club welcomes individuals and teams from all over the world to do gladiatorial battle on eight white podiums in the playing arena. After fighting their way through the rounds, finally a winner takes their seat on the Conker Throne and is crowned with a garland of the little brown nuts as world champion.

Do you have the steady hand and gimlet eye to be all-conquering?

"...it's entirely aggression. There's no defense at all. When you're playing, it's natural to flinch when this thing is being swung at you, especially if it comes very close to your knuckles. The best thing to do is look away and think of England or something else."
Ashton Conker Club secretary John Hadman

Aim of the game

Smash your opponent's conker to smithereens! To do this, the conker must have a hole bored through it and then be threaded onto a knotted string at least 25 cm (10 in.) long. Wrap the loose end of the string through your fingers and clenched palm. It should feel like you are holding a swingable little weapon. Now you and your opponent will take turns to try to hit each other's conker.

The winner of a coin toss decides to either start hitting or start receiving blows. The receiver must hang their conker up ready for the first strike. As striker, you get three swipes in each round, and then it's your turn to be hit. The game continues until one conker is shattered completely off its string. The remaining nut, however battered, is the winner.

The championships have separate Men's, Ladies' and Junior divisions. Teams are also welcome. Juniors can sign up on the day, but everyone else should apply to the organizers in advance.

How to win

Traditionally there are many ways of sneakily hardening your conker before a contest. These include boiling the conkers in vinegar or salt water, soaking in paraffin, baking them, coating them with nail polish and filling them with resin or glue. However, the World Conker Championships supplies the conkers pre-drilled and laced to prevent such naughtiness and so ensure fair play.

Did you know? It was once thought that conkers made horses' coats shinier – hence "horse chestnuts." In reality, the seeds are poisonous to horses. In the two World Wars, the British Government asked children to collect horse chestnuts and donate them. The starch in the seeds was used to make acetone to help in the production of cordite, an explosive used in armaments.

"There are many underhanded ways of making your conker harder. The best is to pass it through a pig. The conker will harden by soaking in its stomach juices. Then you search through the pig's waste to find the conker."

Two-times World Conker
Champion Charlie Bray

63 | GURNING

Better hope the wind doesn't change

Making silly faces is something we all master in our first year at school. World championship gurning, however, takes the activity to a whole new level. To start with, the activity's premier event comes with a prodigious amount of history behind it. Contests in gurning – or making faces – are a longstanding English tradition. The most famous one takes place during the Egremont Crab Fair, a celebration that was given its Royal Charter by King Henry III in 1267 – that's 300 years before Shakespeare was born! The Crab Fair is in fact one of the oldest fairs in the world.

Do you have the stranger-startling looks to grimace your way into history?

It takes place on the third Saturday in September and features several quirky events, including greasy-pole climbing, Cumberland & Westmorland wrestling and the world-famous "gurning."

To gurn means to "snarl like a dog, look savage, distort the countenance," and the rules are simple – pull your ugliest and most outrageous face. You have to do this after putting your head through a horse collar, which focuses the crowd's attention on your face and adds to the comedy value of the expression that you pull. This is technically known as "gurnin' through a braffin."

How to gurn

Practice is key. One winning gurning move is the raising of the lower jaw up and over the upper jaw. However, if you have your own teeth you may find that they get in the way of a really good lip-over-the nose move. Some elderly and toothless gurners have been able to engulf their whole nose with their jaw. So, if you're serious about this sport, you might have to take some remedial action in this area. Peter Jackman, a four-time world champion gurner famous for his "Bela Lugosi" expression actually had all his remaining teeth extracted so that he could truly excel at his chosen discipline.

Did you know? The Crab Fair is not named after crabs, the sea creatures, but crab apples. The celebration is held after harvest time, and the Lord of Egremont started a tradition of giving away recently picked crab apples, lending the fair its name.

A grass roots sport

Motorsports champions enjoy fame and fortune, and their job is an adrenaline rush in itself. NASCAR and Formula One cars have outrageous speed and style, but they are rather expensive and tricky to get your hands on. A Formula One car's steering wheel costs more than your average family sedan and a whole car would cost you at least $8 million. Lawnmowers, however, are available to those of us on a more modest budget.

Lawnmower racing began in 1973 when Irishman Jim Gavin and a few friends were enjoying a liquid lunch in The Cricketers Arms in Wisborough Green, West Sussex. Jim liked rallying, but hated the corporate involvement and professionalism that was coming into the sport. He wanted to create a new, cheap and cheerful motorsport that anyone could try. Looking out across the village green, he saw the groundskeeper mowing the cricket pitch and slowly put down his pint – "Let's race them!" he said to his friends. And so they did, with about eighty mowers turning up for the inaugural race.

The sport has a packed calendar of events, particularly in Britain, where the World Championship takes place over a two-day race weekend. This features heats throughout both days, and all points count towards the final tally to decide the world champion. There is also the very popular twelve-hour Endurance Race that starts at 8 pm on a summer Saturday night and finishes at 8 am on the Sunday morning. Each mower is raced by a team of three drivers.

Although lawnmower racing is a fun sport, competition can be tough. Former Formula One legend Sir Stirling Moss has won the British Grand Prix and the annual twelve-hour race. Derek Bell, five-time Le Mans winner and two-time World Sports Car Champion, has won the twelve-hour twice. Oliver Reed, the late actor, lived in West Sussex and regularly entered a team.

The perfect way to prove you are a cut above the rest.

Revved up and raring to go

There are four different classes of racing machine, and it's best to decide which one you want to race in. Each group has a different size and class of engine, with "Group 3" being the fastest – they can reach 80 km/h (50 mph). You will need to buy a lawnmower and get it homologated by the sport's official team. This makes sure that there aren't any unfairly souped-up machines out there, so there is a level playing field (and it usually really is a field) for everyone. Although you can't modify the engine, you can change the gearing, usually by altering the belt pulleys, to make the machine go faster. Finally, lawnmower racing isn't actually a practical way to cut your grass – your mower's blades must be removed for safety purposes.

Mixed mental and martial arts

Chess requires high levels of mental dexterity and concentration. Being battered about the head by someone else's gloved fists tends to diminish those very attributes. Which is what makes chessboxing such a fascinating fighting sport.

The hybrid event was created by Iepe Rubingh, a Dutch performance artist. It soon moved beyond a performance in his art show to be embraced by strategically minded pugilists as a competitive sport.

There are eleven 3-minute rounds in a chessboxing bout, six of chess and five of boxing. What makes it so tricky is that the chess and boxing rounds alternate – no sooner have you been smashed half-insensible than you have to sit down and start thinking about the benefits of playing the Sicilian Defense against the King's Indian attack.

If neither chessboxer wins in regulation time and the chess game is a draw, the fighter who is ahead on boxing points wins the chessboxing bout.

Judging by the top athletes' physiques, most are boxers who play a little chess on the side, rather than chess grandmasters who happen to have pulled on a pair of gloves. That said, you should be strong in both disciplines to compete at the top level. You will need to have attained a chess Elo rating of 1,600 (at least as good as a competent chess club player) and must have fought at least fifty amateur bouts in boxing or another martial art.

Knight to Queen's uppercut four.

How to win a match

There are several ways that you can win a chessboxing bout:

- **Knockout**
  (boxing rounds)

- **Checkmate**
  (chess rounds)

- **Technical Knockout**
  (boxing rounds)

- **Your opponent exceeds the**
  time limit (chess rounds)

- **Your opponent is disqualified**
  (chess or boxing rounds)

- **Your opponent resigns**
  (chess or boxing rounds)

Stack up or pack up

Sport stacking (also known as speed stacking) was founded in California by Wayne Godinet, a Boys & Girls Club leader. Lots of the kids he looked after didn't like playing traditional ball sports, so he wanted to create an activity that would be fast-moving, competitive, simple and that wouldn't require lots of expensive equipment. Godinet came up with the idea of stacking cups against the clock – and the kids loved it.

How to play

All you have to do is build up pyramid stacks of cups and then de-stack them again. To learn, you will need to get some special plastic sport stacking cups, which are easier to grip and have holes in the base to make play faster. There are three main events in the official championship:

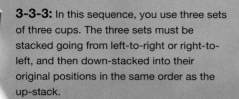

3-3-3: In this sequence, you use three sets of three cups. The three sets must be stacked going from left-to-right or right-to-left, and then down-stacked into their original positions in the same order as the up-stack.

3-6-3: This sequence is similar to the 3-3-3, except a six-stack replaces the three-stack in the middle. Each pile of cups is stacked up from left-to-right or right-to-left, and the down-stack occurs in the same order.

Cycle: In this sequence, you use twelve cups, stacking them in the following order: a 3-6-3 stack, a 6-6 stack (two pyramids of six cups stacked up and down into one containing all twelve cups) and a 1-10-1 stack (a pyramid of ten cups in the middle), finishing in a down-stacked 3-6-3.

You can do sport stacking on your own or in a team. Doubles and four-player relays are particularly popular. Most sport stacking competitions are aimed at youths, but there are some adult contests. The 2016 All-Around World Sport Stacking Champion was Chan Keng Ian from Malaysia, with a 9.065 second combined time. He also won the 2015 Asian Open Grand Champion. Chang had won both championships by the time he was 11 years old.

A fast-moving sport to try your hand at.

Put your rivals in a spin

The yo-yo was invented by the Ancient Greeks around 500 BC, but it only exploded into worldwide popularity in the 1920s. The first world championship was held in London in 1932 and was won by famous Canadian yo-yoer Harvey Lowe. He made a career out of his mastery of the toy, but the World Yo-Yo Contest only became an annual event in 1992, when it was re-established in Montreal. This is now the sport's headline event, with the clout and cachet to crown the ultimate champions for the year. It attracts more than 1,000 yo-yo players from over thirty countries and now moves between host cities in North America, Europe and Asia.

Japan is the nation to beat. In the last twenty-two years it has won seventy-one world titles. The U.S. is the next most successful country, with twenty-six world crowns. The nimble-fingered Shinji Saito is the most decorated yo-yoer of all-time with thirteen world titles.

A yo-yo competition has two parts: compulsory tricks and freestyle. Compulsory tricks (also known as a trick ladder) are predetermined by officials, and competitors have two attempts to pull them off and rand in the points. Freestyle is as it sounds – each yo-yoer delivers an original routine set to music. The panel of judges will score it based on difficulty of the tricks, synchronization with the music and artistic performance.

Top yo-yoers are extraordinarily dexterous and may have thousands of intricate tricks up their sleeves. The national champions from accredited countries automatically earn a spot in the preliminary rounds of the championship, and the outright champion automatically gets a place in the following year's final. However, the world championship is still open to everyone via the Wild Card round. This gives non-seeded players 30 seconds to shine and earn one of the few places on offer in the preliminary round.

This lasts 1 minute, and the best performers go on through to the semi-final, in which you are allowed 1 minute 30 seconds to perform. In the grand final you have 3 minutes to lay down an inspiring and unforgettable routine of tricks.

No sport
has more
ups and
downs.

171

> **"The Japanese are super into yo-yo. They're all into precision. Their tricks … they have them down to almost a science."**
>
> Zach Gormley, 2015 world champion

Competitive categories

There are six divisions in which you can earn your "World Yo-Yo Champion" title, and they require different skills and tricks.

1A **Single Hand String Trick** You use a long spinning yo-yo to perform tricks that typically require manipulation of the string.

2A **Two Hands Looping Trick** You use two yo-yos simultaneously to perform reciprocating or looping maneuvers.

3A **Two Hands String Trick** You use two long spinning yo-yos and perform tricks with both simultaneously.

4A **Offstring** You use an offstring yo-yo, often releasing the yo-yo into the air and attempting to catch it on the string.

5A **Counterweight** You use a yo-yo with a counterweight on the other end of the string, rather than having it attached to your finger.

AP **Artistic Performance** You use any type of yo-yo or other prop for an open-ended performance which emphasizes choreography and stage presence.

WHERE FLORIDA, U.S. | **SINCE** 1980s
USEFUL EQUIPMENT SQUEEGEE, CHAMOIS

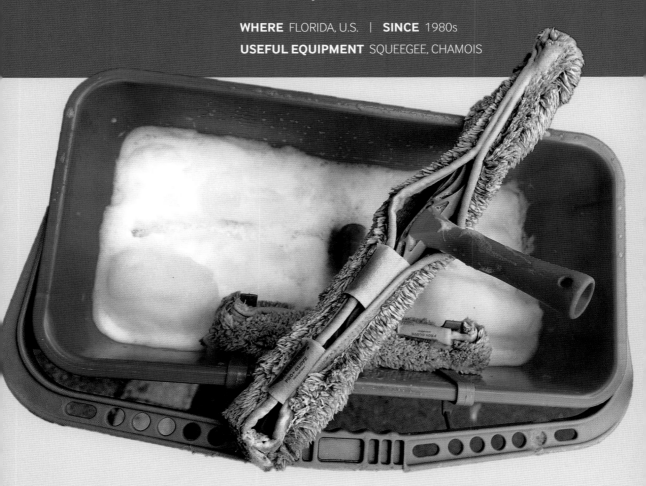

"...we have pretty much been practicing every day. A gym membership is also advantageous: body control and conditioning are essential."

Ivan Pleinadius on training Marianne and Ivan, the 2015 World Window Cleaning Champions (Speed Cleaning Division)

Clearly the best

Going super quickly is often the problem with window cleaners. A couple of swipes and a swoop and they're done – can they really have cleaned it properly? Well, apparently so, because the World Window Cleaning Championship is not just about raw speed – every square inch of every pane of glass has to be gleaming clean and smear-free. There are two main categories at the championships: "speed cleaning" and "the medley."

Speed cleaning

You have to clean a row of windows as quickly as possible without leaving a single smudge or smear. There are three glass windows measuring 1.14-m (45-in.) square. Each window has a 5-cm (2-in.) sill. The windows are dry at the start of the contest.

You must use a 300-cm (1-ft) squeegee with a brand-new rubber and a fixed handle, which is supplied by the organizers. Swivel squeegees or any modified tools are not allowed. You have a maximum of 9 l (2.5 gal) of water. You will also be supplied with a chamois for finishing.

You must wet, soap and clean the full area of all three windows. You then have to finish your windows to clear all smears, streaks and water residue.

Each smear incurs a half-second penalty. A dirty sill will incur a one-second penalty.

The medley

In this contest, you have to clean a selection of windows that range in size from 23 cm by 31 cm (9 in. by 12 in.) to 119 cm by 194 cm (47 in. by 76.5 in.). At least two of these are set up above arm's reach and must be cleaned using a pole. One of these upper windows has an extra-deep sill.

The contest foreman will count you down – 3, 2, 1, GO! Your tools start in your bucket. You must wipe, sponge and clean all windows within reach, then use your pole for the upper windows.

Touching up of the windows is not allowed. However, you may re-clean any windows that you are not happy with. You can use your chamois, rags or sponges to clean your squeegee. Please note: unsportsmanlike conduct is grounds for disqualification. This includes the throwing of tools, excessive intoxication and verbal abuse of others. It seems that window cleaners are passionate about their craft...

Can you wipe the smile off your opponent's face?

Splash into the sludge

If you haven't yet enjoyed their delicious taste and texture, "grits" are made from ground corn boiled into a gloop, and are a very popular breakfast dish in the southern U.S. They also make for a spectacularly messy world championship thanks to the new sport of grits rolling.

The aim of the game is to collect as great a weight of grits onto your person as possible. Twenty-seven cases of the savory foodstuff are poured into an inflatable tub. The grits are ready for rolling in when the stirring paddle stands straight up in the huge porridgey puddle. You then have 10 seconds to dive in and collect as much of the grits as you can. You will be weighed before and after your rolls. The winner earns $200 prize money and a good hose-down.

Top tactics

Rolling in the grits to make them adhere to your clothing is the basic move. But you can also scoop them into your clothing; many competitors wear sweatpants, hoodies and other voluminous articles, often with the wrists and ankles taped shut. You can also swallow the grits or stash them in your pockets. Advanced rollers have been known to roughly shampoo their hair before the event – the grits stick

Did you know? "Grits" comes from the Old English word "grytt," meaning coarse meal. The exact recipe for competitive grits changes depending on the weather on competition day. The hotter the sun, the more water needed in the mix. In 2015, the contest was delayed by 25 minutes while the grits cooled enough to allow rolling.

better. And if your sweatpants are old and fuzzy on the inside – even better for grit-gripping.

You'll have to raise your game if you want to beat the locals: the town of St. George first held the competition because the local Piggly Wiggly supermarket had worked out that its citizens were the nation's greatest grits consumers. The world record, held by Tiffany McGirr, is an impressive 30 kg (66 lb).

Should you be crowned world champion, the only potential downside is that you might not be able to hear the cheers of the crowd, thanks to all the grits in your ears.

Win or lose, you'll never look at breakfast in the same way again.

Sole champion

It's fair to say that unicycling is a niche discipline within the broader sport of cycling. Within unicycling, cross-country is a niche discipline, and mountain unicycling, or "muni" as it is known to its adherents, is an even more specialized form. And the extraordinary skills, stamina, and crazy ambition needed to become a world champion of such an event are gifted to very, very few people.

At first glance it might seem that mountain unicyclists are simply making things unnecessarily difficult for themselves. Mountain biking is hard enough on two wheels; why do away with one of those wheels? What's next – pogo-stick skiing?

But the difficulty is part of the attraction. In the world of extreme sports there are far fewer people who have ridden a double black diamond mountain bike downhill trail on a unicycle than have done a BASE jump or ridden a tube at the fearsome Mavericks surf break. So those who like unicycling REALLY do love it, and the sport certainly presents a unique challenge that, by rising up to it, gives a unique kind of thrill.

Muni is done on the same off-road terrain as normal mountain biking, including in wild country and highly technical singletrack. However, as unicycles have no freewheel, they can only go as fast as a rider's legs permit, even on descent. This means the rider must have the strength to remain in total control at all times. A rock-solid core and exceptional balance are essential. Downhill unicycles feature thick, heavy-duty tires, rugged frames and high-performance hubs. Some models have brakes and two-gear hubs.

No handlebars and no fear...

The one that matters

Muni's premier laurels are fought for at Unicon, unicycling's hottest event. There are four muni disciplines in the world championships:

Cross-country – An off-road race where waves of unicyclists ride along a rugged course of uphill, downhill and long, moderate-difficulty flat sections. First past the post wins.

Downhill – An off-road race where waves of unicyclists ride downhill on a rugged slope of high difficulty. First past the post wins.

Uphill – An off-road race where waves of unicyclists ride uphill on a rugged slope of high difficulty. First past the post wins.

Cyclocross – A race over a set time around a mountain circuit with artificial obstacles, which can be overcome by dismounting. The rider who completes most laps is the winner.

"One of the best things about a unicycle is that it's so minimal that you forget it's even there – it becomes an extension of your body as you twist back and forth to roll around rocks and roots."

Kris Holm, world trials champion and
legendary mountain unicyclist

Four large oak logs are all that stand between you and history.

Chop against the clock

You'll need strong shoulders and hands like leather to master this sport. You have to hack your way through four massive logs using different woodsman skills. For the first log you use a heavy chainsaw – this is the easy round. Then, using an axe, you must chop through a log beneath your feet (being very careful not to take any of your own toes off). After that you move onto the razor-sharp long handsaw, and finally the axe again to chop through a standing log.

The current world-record holder, Australia's Brad Delosa, managed all this in less than fifty-eight seconds.

Chopping checklist

Grip – your left hand should be 2 cm (1 in.) from the bottom of the handle. This hand delivers nearly all the control. Your right hand should be three-quarters of the way up towards the axe head. This hand slides during the blow and is more of a level that guides the axe head to hit in the right place.

Backswing – give the axe head as much time in the air as possible to allow the angles to come together perfectly. Hitting too quickly will cost you power.

The downstroke – aim to hit through the wood, rather than just hitting and stopping.

Training – to work on your muscles and build your balance skills, practice turning over tractor tires.

"Your core, your legs and your arms come together as one to get as much power out of your body and onto the block as possible."

Brad Delosa

181

Do a mean version of *Bohemian Rhapsody?* Prove it.

Sing it to win it

Karaoke isn't just for bachelorette parties and work nights out that you'd rather forget in the morning. It could also be your open door to world championship glory.

The World Karaoke Championship is officially the biggest amateur singing competition in the world, and it's been making people's diva dreams come true since 2003.

How to enter

Your first step is to sing in your home country's national trials. If – sorry, when – you win that, you will get a paid trip to represent your nation in the world championship final. The only qualifying conditions are that you are over 18 and are not paid to sing – amateurs only.

Time to take the stage

You will have to sing in four separate rounds over three days. The last man and woman standing will be crowned as world champions! The tournament has a catalogue of over 100,000 songs, so there's bound to be something that suits your style. Yes, *Bohemian Rhapsody* is in there…

There's no sport in the world that's more fun to train for, that's for sure.

In vino veritas

Can you tell a Chablis from a Sancerre? A French Merlot from an Argentinian Malbec? Or do you just want a good reason to savor lots and lots of very fine wine?

The World Wine Tasting Championship isn't a competition to decide which wines are the best, but how good tasters are at identifying different grapes and homelands. The competition is held in a different wine-growing part of France every year – in 2015, the host was southern Rhône's Châteauneuf-du-Pape – and twenty international teams are invited to compete.

The twelve wines are divided evenly into six white and six red varieties. In 2015, five of these were from France, including a Château Climens 2008 (a Sauternes) and the 2007 Châteauneuf-du-Pape. International wines included a 2013 New Zealand Sauvignon Blanc from Te Mata in Hawke's Bay and a 2011 Friedrich Becker Sonnenberg Riesling from Germany. Some are very tricky: no team identified the Malvasia from Croatia, and only the Belgians correctly called the Greek Assyrtiko. The mighty French team was eventually humbled, as the event was won by Spain, with Belgium in second place and Sweden in third. The U.S. team came last.

They all taste good to me

Your five-person squad of vino mavens has to identify the twelve very varied wines in a blind taste test. Your palates must pinpoint:

the wines' countries of origin

the grape varieties used

the appellations

the vintages

And you have to do it all before you get too sloshed to care. It is a demanding challenge because you must agree as a team on each of the above factors, meaning that team dynamics can play a large part in performance.

The best thing of all is that if you do win, you are in the absolutely ideal place to start celebrating.

"We were confident at the start but then it became complicated. We had disagreements (over identifying wines) and often had to reach a compromise."

Christophe Dantzenberg, member of the last-placed U.S. team

"There was no trap. But some wines are not easy to identify, like Croatian or Greek ones."

Philippe de Cantenac, event organizer

185

Go low on the snow

If skiing and snowboarding have always seemed a little... well... complicated, then it could very well be that shovel racing is the ideal winter sport for you. Get a shovel, sit on it, whoosh down a mountain – that's pretty much all there is to it. Oh, and falling off. There's an awful lot of that, too.

A history of speed skidding

The sport was born in New Mexico's ski resorts in the 1970s, when staff working on the ski tows and trails got the knack of using their snow shovels as sleds to zoom around the mountains. Why they didn't just use skis like every other sensible person has not been recorded.

The craziness does have a few rules

You must use a standard-issue shovel only; modified shovels are not allowed. However, you can wax your shovel and put tape on the handle for a bit of extra grip. Be careful how much wax you put on though, as shovels don't need much encouragement to go quickly. Elite shovel racers can top 112 km/h (70 mph).

Your time from start to finish is timed electronically to a thousandth of a second. You should note that you and your shovel have to cross the line together; your time does not count if you fall off and happen to skid down the mountain separately.

Top tip

Don't worry if you happen to cause an avalanche – with your shovel to hand you should easily be able to dig yourself out.

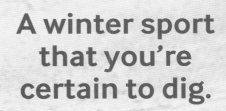

A winter sport that you're certain to dig.

Ready, steady, roach

Seeing a roach scurry across the floor is normally a cause of revulsion, which sees you reaching for the nearest weapon to swat it with. However, there is one day of the year when it could be a cause for jubilation, which sees you reaching for the nearest beer to celebrate with.

On Australia Day (26 January), cockroach fever grips the city of Brisbane. For it is here that you can witness what has been called "the greatest gathering of thoroughbred cockroaches in the world" – the Gold Cup at the Story Bridge Hotel.

This is the original and still the greatest event in the world's cockroach-racing calendar.

The race itself is simple, but terrifically exciting. The race arena is a ring of 6 m (20 ft) in diameter. At the start of the race, the roaches are held in glass bottles to prevent them from running off under the fridge. On the referee's command they are released into the middle of the ring. The cockroach that reaches the edge of the ring first is the winner. Well, its owner is – the cockroaches don't have a clue what's going on.

Hit the lights and watch them scatter – hopefully in the right direction.

Did you know? As scurrying insects go, cockroaches are second only to the tiger beetle in flat-out speed. A cockroach can move at a rate of fifty body lengths per second. If Usain Bolt were a cockroach (which is rather an unpleasant mental image, now we think about it), he'd run the 100 m in a second and would top 322 km/h (200 mph).

"I have been practicing for days at home. I have my own stag, which I've been listening to."

Immo Ortlepp, German champion

It's time to do your best wild animal impression.

Your invitation to the stag party

At the World Deer Calling Championship, you have to use horns, pipes, plastic tubes, shells or simply your own vocal chords to imitate a bellowing stag as accurately as possible.

The competition was born out of a traditional practice still used by farmers and hunters. The stag-like noises calm the stags, allowing a closer approach on foot.

How to hoof it

It's not just a matter of going up on stage and bellowing. This is a subtle art, and you must be able to imitate the deer in several states, including:

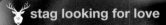 **stag looking for love**

stag victorious after a fight

 **stag exhausted after a long night's mating**

You may want to join the contestants who get into the spirit of the event by dressing in traditional German lederhosen. Not that this will impress the judges, all veteran hunters. They take their job extremely seriously, and sit sequestered behind a screen so that they can concentrate fully on evaluating the deer-ness of the sounds you make.

191

The excitement is in tents.

"It's very interesting to see the different techniques that people use when erecting a tent but, at the end of the day, it all comes down to good teamwork."

Matt Clark, competition judge

Top pitching tips

- Use the instructions! Of course it's not as macho, but 95 percent of people ignore the instructions, and if you want to be a champ you should be one of the 5 percent who read them.
- Teamwork is important and absolutely vital on the larger tents – one person can't erect them solo. Communication is everything.
- Location, location, location. When you're practicing watch out for rocks, bogs, sheep droppings, ants' nests – anything that could slow you down.
- Secure all guy ropes. They aren't a nice extra, but an integral part of the tent's structure, as planned by its designer. They should be taut and at the correct angle.

Gimme shelter

If you've ever had to put up a family tent in a thrashing downpour, when the mosquitoes are biting and the kids are complaining, you may not want to repeat the experience ever again. However, if your friends were amazed at how soon after arriving at a music festival you had pitched and were heading off to the bar, this could be the event for you.

It started as a bit of fun at an outdoors equipment trade show, but the World Tent Pitching Championship has become a crowd-pulling sensation in its own right. The action is fast, entertaining and often amusingly shouty.

The ground(sheet) rules

The championship is fought for by two-person teams. There are different disciplines, from a simple two-person tent, to multiple tent challenges involving a selection of family and technical mountaineering tents. After several audience members at an early contest pointed out that indoor pitching was less of a challenge, the organizers brought along wind and rain machines in pursuit of an authentic challenge (although they refrained from releasing clouds of biting insects).

You can book your place at the world championships by winning a qualifying competition at one of the smaller outdoor shows. Or, you can try your luck in the heats at the main event itself. You'll pick up a penalty for every missing peg and any guy ropes that aren't twanging-tight.

If you do triumph, you will win a £1,000 ($1,400) camping trip of a lifetime, camping equipment and, even better, the Golden Mallet Trophy.

Put a spring in your step

This sport leapt into public awareness in the early 2000s when some young stunt-lovers tried doing tricks on traditional steel-sprung pogo sticks. They were able to get a bit of air, but the sport was far from spectacular. However, it really took off in 2004, when a new stick was introduced that had giant rubber "elastomers" instead of a steel spring. This gave bounces a stretchy, bungee-jumping feel. Within a year, extreme pogo – or Xpogo – practitioners were landing full backflips and other spectacular stunts.

Trying it out

An extreme pogo stick is very different from the sedate hopping instrument you may find in your attic. It's a fully primed and powerful springing machine that will flip you heavenwards in a heartbeat. If you want to try it out, you could go to Pogopalooza and pop along to the Free Jump/Clinic, where an expert will help get you started. From there, the sky's your limit.

The official world championship is a series of events known as Pogopalooza. At championship level, there are three main categories in which you can triumph:

Big Air – You have to bounce around a specially designed obstacle course with boxes, ramps and steps.

Best Trick – The aim is to pull off as many bouncingly brilliant stunts as you can. Tricks can include the back flip, front flip, scissor kick, 360 leapfrog and the peg stall.

High Jump – Exactly what you might think – just how high a bar can you clear? The current world record is 2.97 m (9.7 ft).

Be prepared for ups and downs.

195

The cutting edge of art.

Ready for the chop

If you're lucky enough to live in a forest, you can start practicing for world domination in the fast and frantic art of chainsaw carving. You'll probably need to take a few lessons from an expert, as your artistic tool is also a potential killing machine. Carvers use chainsaws with special narrow blades and short teeth so that the end of the saw can be used for detailed work without "kicking" off the wood.

Even for the experts, chainsaw carving is noisy and messy, but the results can be spectacular and beautiful. In 2011, English chainsaw artist Matthew Crabb carved the largest wooden statue of the Virgin Mary in the world, at 9 m (29.5 ft) high. He expressed the difficulty of the art: "It is so hard to know whether you are on the right track... If you get something wrong, there is no going back."

Expert carving tip

Eyes are tricky things to even draw with pencil and paper, never mind carve out of wood with a whirring saw blade. Novices often run into a lot of trouble by starting to carve the outside of the eye first, beginning with the eyelids. Then they try to add in the eye socket, any wrinkles and finally do the eyeballs. Often they find that they have run out of space, and the eyeball is either squished in or ends up looking "piggy." Instead, reverse the process and start carving the eyeball first. You can then add in the eyelid, wrinkles and other textures. Your eyeball might seem big at first, but this is much easier to adjust.

197

Timber...!

Lumberjacks have to be very careful about where they bring their trees down, and they can become very skillful indeed at hitting a mark. The World Logging Championship celebrates this expertise, giving contestants a mere three minutes to fell a tree and land it as closely as possible to a marker.

Penalty points will be incurred if the logger runs out of time, and each felling is also judged on how far (in centimeters) the tree lands from the marker, the depth and angle of the undercut, and the height difference between the directional cut and the hinge between the two cuts that are needed to bring the tree down (rounded to the nearest millimeter).

Felling a tree in the right direction

Most trees want to fall in one particular direction. The direction of their lean, the size and shape of their branches, and the ground conditions will all affect this natural fall direction.

You can, to some extent, make a tree fall in a different way. But this requires professional expertise and carries greater risk. You should always fell dead or decayed trees in the easiest direction.

The basic idea of the felling is that you are making a hinge in the trunk that will steer the tree to the ground. First, you make a "directional cut" to remove a wedge-shaped chunk on the same side you want the tree to fall. Now make the "felling cut" horizontally in from the opposite side. You should leave a hinge of about 3 cm (1.2 in.), depending on the tree girth. You may need to insert a wedge in the felling cut to prevent the tree from trapping the bar of your saw, and to help set the tree on its way.

I'm a lumberjack and I'm okay...

Kilt – check, haggis –
check, whisky – check.
Let's go!

Blow your rivals away

Given that bagpiping has historically been used by the Scots as a means of terrifying the enemy on the battlefield, you might think that all you have to do is make as loud and raucous a racket as possible. And how hard can that be?

Very hard indeed, is the short answer. Learning the bagpipes may feel like you're wrestling an unruly octopus at first, but if you're good at multitasking, the bagpipes could very well be your instrument. When you're playing a guitar, one hand frets the

notes, the other strums or picks the strings. Two things in motion. But with the bagpipes, both your hands are playing notes as your mouth blows like fury into a bag that you constantly squeeze with your arm. That's four things to manage at once, while your brain is trying to remember the tune and your foot is tapping the rhythm.

The easiest way to learn bagpiping is to join a pipe band, but you can also become a champion by playing solo. The World Solo Amateur Piping Competition and the World Pipe Band

Championships both take place every summer in Glasgow, the biggest city in Scotland.

Usually in the competition you'll perform an "MSR," a set of three traditional types of tune: a March, a Strathspey and a Reel. The Medley is free choice and you and your band will play an original medley of your own. This should be as inventive as possible, including jigs and slow airs, and with different time signatures.

The good news is that different grades compete at "The Worlds," as the Glasgow championships are known. The very best players are Grade 1, and you're looking at years of practice if you want to triumph here. But there are also Grades 2, 3A, 3B, 4A and 4B, and under-18s Grades – the Juvenile and Novice Juvenile bands. So, if you're a new, young player, you can pipe your heart out in Novice Juveniles and become a valid world champion.

You can also become a champion by topping your country's bagpiping league. Bagpiping associations designate "sanctioned" contests throughout the bagpiping event year, and your scores in at least six of these will be counted to determine the "Champion Supreme" for each grade.

Finally, you don't *have* to wear a kilt, but you really should. Not only will it get you in the bagpiping mood, it's terrific fun!

A sport that's going downhill fast

The luge is a winter sport that is basically sledding down a steep, curving ice track at lunatic speeds. Which makes street luge basically sledding down a steep, curving asphalt road. At lunatic speeds. You lie on what is little more than a tray with wheels and launch yourself down the steepest street you can find. Ideally, you should ensure there is no other traffic on the road.

Street luge's riding low-lying position is very aerodynamically efficient. The axles and wheels are designed for raw speed, rather than any ability to pull off stunts. This means that you can reach speeds of up to 157 km/h (97 mph) and pull a centripetal acceleration of up to 5g on the tightest corners.

"Dude, I have an awesome idea"

Downhill skateboarders in California realized that the best way to get pure speed out of their skateboards was to lie on them. They couldn't see where they were going but, hey, they were getting there quickly. In the 1980s and 90s this developed into a whole new extreme sport, and the world title has been vigorously contended ever since.

There are two basic styles: classic luge and street luge. Classic boards are more like large skateboards and have smaller wheels. This style is also known as buttboard. Street luge boards have larger wheels, a broader and longer base and more features. There are several elements that all street luge boards must have:

- lean-activated steering skateboard-style trucks
- front and rear padding
- length, width and weight restrictions
  – details depend on the sanctioning body
- no parts that enclose the rider's body
- absolutely no mechanical brakes

Yep, you read that right – no mechanical brakes.

Races are usually held on mountain roads, but city streets do feature if they can be closed off. Trucks and street lugers are not good bedfellows. Courses can be up to 5 km (3 miles) long, have a variety of swooping or severe turns, and vary in layout (number and severity of turns). There are several very popular racing formats:

- single elimination with two, four or six racers at a time
- double elimination with two, four or six racers at a time
- timed trials
- no elimination points system (points for each finishing position in several heats)
- mass runs, with up to twenty racers at a time (positions are decided by the order in which they cross the finish line)

You may be lying
down, but you won't be
dropping off to sleep.

"You have bottomless boats, you step inside the boats and you run in the sands with them down to the marker and back. It's like Fred Flintstone and his car in The Flintstones."

Eleanor Dennis, commodore of the Henley-on-Todd regatta

Turning sailing on its head down under.

No buoyancy, no problem

A regatta is a chance for rowers and sailors to prove their skills and find out who will be crowned champion. One of the world's largest and most popular such events is the Henley regatta, which has been held on the River Thames in England since 1839.

The town of Alice Springs also has a famous regatta, which has been held on the Todd River since 1962. It was modelled on its English forebear, with one crucial difference: the Todd River has no water.

The Henley-on-Todd is the world's premier (and only) dry riverbed regatta. A huge flotilla of crafts takes to the non-existent water, including rowing boats, canoes and yachts. Victory here will certainly see you going down in dusty history.

Sea legs not required

As there is no water, you don't need sailing skills. Just a bottomless boat – ideally decorated in an amusing fashion – and a crew with good running skills.

Did you know? The event has been "washed out" once in fifty years, when heavy rains actually caused the normally absent Todd River to make a rare appearance.

84 | POWERSLIDING

Revved up and ready

To the uninitiated, powersliding might just look like driving around a corner so fast that your back tires burn themselves into smoky oblivion. But there is a very subtle and skillful art to this fast-growing niche motorsport.

What is it?

Drifting has revved its way into popular culture thanks to the *Fast and the Furious* movies, but powersliding is not quite the same as drifting. They are both types of controlled oversteer, but in a powerslide you use the momentum of the car coming through the corner to slide. In a drift, you start your car sliding before entering the corner. In other words, a powerslide

You'll need the right line, lots of power and your wheels pointing the wrong way.

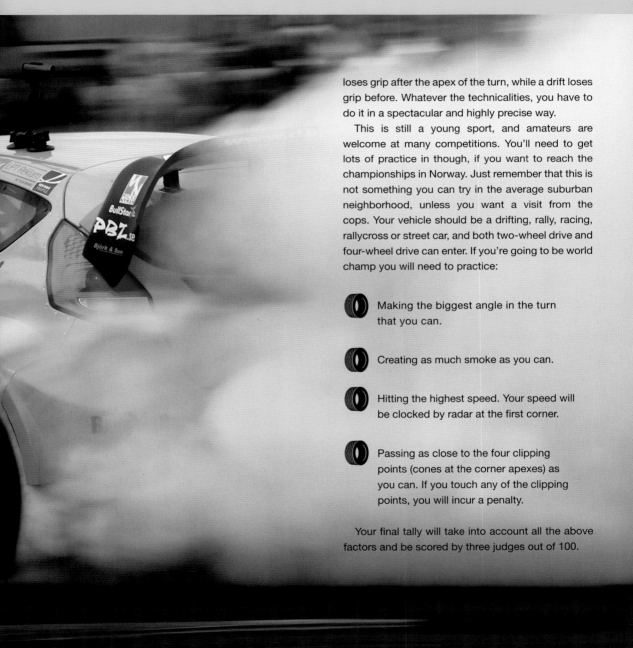

loses grip after the apex of the turn, while a drift loses grip before. Whatever the technicalities, you have to do it in a spectacular and highly precise way.

This is still a young sport, and amateurs are welcome at many competitions. You'll need to get lots of practice in though, if you want to reach the championships in Norway. Just remember that this is not something you can try in the average suburban neighborhood, unless you want a visit from the cops. Your vehicle should be a drifting, rally, racing, rallycross or street car, and both two-wheel drive and four-wheel drive can enter. If you're going to be world champ you will need to practice:

Making the biggest angle in the turn that you can.

Creating as much smoke as you can.

Hitting the highest speed. Your speed will be clocked by radar at the first corner.

Passing as close to the four clipping points (cones at the corner apexes) as you can. If you touch any of the clipping points, you will incur a penalty.

Your final tally will take into account all the above factors and be scored by three judges out of 100.

Mallet-swinging madness

If you're fast on a bike and have ever played hockey, cycle polo could very well be the sport for you. This team game is basically a version of traditional polo, but with bikes instead of wild-eyed horses.

There are two major variations on the basic game – traditional cycle polo and the newer hardcourt bike polo. The traditional form of the game is actually quite old – it was first played in County Wicklow, Ireland, in 1891. The first international match, between Ireland and England, was played in 1901. Cycle polo even made it to the Olympics, as a demonstration sport at the 1908 London games. There are four players per side on the pitch at any one time, and they have a good amount of space to pedal around in – officially the pitch should be 150 m by 100 m (492 ft by 328 ft). However, "a nice big field" is usually good enough. You are equipped with a mallet and helmet and you have to chase after the ball and knock it into the other team's goal. International matches last for thirty minutes divided into four 7.5-minute chukkas.

Since 2007, there has been increased interest in a new, faster, more urban form of the game: hardcourt bike polo. This three-on-three version is played on any smaller, firm-surfaced pitch that can be found. Tennis courts, five-on-five soccer pitches, street-hockey rinks and basketball courts have all been used.

Like normal polo, just without the neighing and the horse poop.

How to play hardcourt

Here are the main hardcourt rules you need to know:

- The game starts with a frenetic "joust" – the players line up behind their own goals while the ball is placed center court. The referee starts a countdown, and when he finishes both teams charge full speed to get the ball.

- Matches are played as the first to five points or to a fifteen-minute time limit if the game is low scoring. There are no chukkas.

- Putting your foot down is a big no-no. This is called a "dab," and if you do this you must "tap out" by riding to midcourt and hitting a special area with your mallet.

- You can only score by hitting the ball across the goal line with the narrow end of the mallet – this is called a "shot." Hitting with the wide part of the mallet head is called a "shuffle," and cannot be used to score.

Hardcourt bike polo is particularly popular in the U.S., but there are also strong national championships in Australia, New Zealand, the United Kingdom and Germany. The world championships have been held every year since the first event in Toronto in 2008.

Pimp your ride

You can play with any bike you like, but top players all tend to go for a single-speed bike with a low gear ratio. This offers rapid acceleration and good control on a small court. You may also want to customize your ride with a super-short wheelbase and a longer stem to help you make tight turns. Wheel covers will protect your spokes and act as a block to your opponents. They also look pretty cool.

86 | EGG THROWING

WHERE LINCOLNSHIRE, ENGLAND | **SINCE** 2006
USEFUL EQUIPMENT QUICK HANDS, GOGGLES

Do you have
what it takes to
achieve sporting
egg-cellence?

The yolk's on you

This sport might be better described as "egg catching," since throwing a fresh egg isn't really that hard at all. It's catching the fast-moving and hopelessly fragile projectile at the other end without it smashing all over you that is the tricky part.

Egg throwing is done by teams of two – catchers and tossers. The pairs make their first throw standing 10 m (33 ft) apart. If you drop the egg or break it, you are out! All those who successfully catch their egg go through to the next round. For this, the catchers and tossers step away from each other to widen the throwing distance. In the heats, this process is repeated until five pairs are left. These top five go through to the grand final, where the throwing and spreading goes on until only one pair is left – the world champions!

High standards

If you want to be in with a chance, you will need to work on your technique. The official World Egg Throwing Record was set in 2014 by the brothers Andries and Bauke Jetze Smink with an eggs-traordinary throw of 76.27 m (250.22 ft).

Rules of the range

The organizer supplies all eggs for the competition. They are marked for security purposes and must be broken by the heat or final winner, to prove that they have not been switched or tampered with. Players are not allowed to use any aid when catching or throwing eggs, such as a glove, net or propelling instrument (slings, catapults, modified rocket launchers, etc.).

Eggs-tra ways to glory

As well as the headline event of egg throwing, you can also be crowned champion in the following disciplines:

Egg Static Relay – A team of eleven players stands along a 100-m (328-ft) long route. Players may not move more than 5 m (16.5 ft) from their mark. Twelve eggs are passed one at a time along the line. A broken egg incurs a three-second penalty. Fastest time wins.

Egg Target Throwing – A volunteer stands 7.3 m (24 ft) in front of a thrower who has four eggs. The thrower must hit selected target areas of the volunteer to earn points. Eggs that don't break may be re-thrown.

Russian Egg Roulette – Individual players sit at opposite sides of a table. They don a "Deer Hunter" style bandana for protection. Each is given a tray of six eggs: one will be raw, five will be hard-boiled. The players take it in turn to select an egg and smash it against their forehead. First to find the raw egg loses.

Egg Trebuchet – Teams construct gravity-powered machines based on the ancient trebuchet design. The base should be no larger than 2 m² (21.5 ft²) – these aren't ostrich eggs we're throwing here, people. One team member aims the trebuchet at a set distance. Another team member goes to stand at this point. The trebuchet fires an egg. Points are awarded for striking the target, bonus points if the egg is caught unbroken. The target may move in order to be struck/make a catch. Teams get three eggs at each distance.

87 | QUIZZING

WHERE WORLDWIDE | **SINCE** 2003
USEFUL EQUIPMENT MASSIVE BRAIN

Tonight your
pub quiz,
tomorrow
the world.

No phones allowed

Which chemical element is the main constituent of photographic emulsions? If you don't know that the answer is silver, chances are you aren't going to take the gold.

The World Quizzing Championships itself is Trivial Pursuit times a thousand. Fact fans in venues around the world sit a written test made up of 240 questions, which must be answered in two hours. These cover a wide variety of subjects including sciences, culture, entertainment, history and sports. The test is available in a number of languages.

The questions are hard but fair – a team of judges from the International Quizzing Association spends nine months of the year writing questions that are equally accessible to people anywhere in the world. They start with a first group of 1,500 questions, which will be slowly whittled down by votes to create the 240-question championship set. The questions are gauged for fairness, international accessibility and coverage of a range of subjects, and once selected, they are translated into twelve languages.

Did you know? England is the country to beat – its quizzers have won the competition twelve out of the thirteen times it has been held.

If you're good, there'll be no squopping you.

A nudge and a wink

If you're not strong or fast or super-intelligent, and are despairing of ever becoming a world champion in anything at all, tiddlywinks is the game for you. It has only remained in the public eye because, in 1955, some students at Cambridge University who were just as unathletic as you, got together one dark January night (in a pub, probably) to devise a sport at which they could represent the university. They settled on a then-forgotten Victorian parlor game that involved flipping tiny circular discs into a pot using a slightly larger circular disc.

The game's blend of strategy, skill and quirkiness caught the students' imagination. Within three years, their great rival Oxford University was fielding a team. Then, in 1962, the Oxford University Tiddlywinks Society (OUTS) spent several weeks touring the United States under the sponsorship of Guinness. (It was a hard life being a student in those days.) Their towering tiddlywinking talents stunned the Americans into action, and soon teams were formed at Harvard, Cornell, MIT and many other universities. Tiddlywinks was back on the world sporting map.

How to tiddle your wink

Each player has six "winks" – small round plastic discs of a single color. You place these in one corner of a rectangular felt mat measuring 1.83 m by 0.91 m (6 ft by 3 ft). In the center of the mat there is a pot (always red, for some unknown reason) that is the target of the game. With the other players you then take turns at using your "squidger" (a plastic disc larger than a wink) to press down on the wink and squeeze it into flight. The main aim is to get as many of your winks into the pot as possible. As in pool, when you pot a wink you get an extra shot. However, you can also play a "squop" shot, where you cover an opponent's wink. A squopped wink cannot be played by its owner. And this creates the strategic

complexity of the game – do you shoot for the pot or disable your opponent? Or, in a team game, play a mixed strategy? The game ends when a player pots all his winks (a pot-out), or a pre-specified time limit is reached and the scores are added up.

Outwinking the world

The World Singles Championship has been tiddled for since 1973. To challenge at the world level, a player must win one of the national titles, or finish as the highest-placed home player behind a foreign winner. The three main national competitions are the National Singles, National Pairs, and the Teams of Four. You are also welcome to enter the annual Open Competitions, which in the UK take place in Oxford, Cambridge and London.

Tiddling terminology

There are many specialist shots that you should work on in your practice session:

Boondock – To free a squopped wink by sending it far away, leaving the squopping wink free.

Bristol – Moving a pile of two or more winks as a single unit with one shot. You play this shot holding the squidger at a right angle to its normal plane.

Carnovsky (U.S.)/Penhaligon (UK) – Potting a wink from the baseline.

Gromp – Trying to jump a pile onto another wink.

John Lennon memorial shot – A simultaneous boondock and squop.

Squop – To play a wink so that it lands on another wink.

Tiddlies – Points added up to work out the winning winkers in a tiddlywinks game.

Hold on tight

Imagine the pole vault, but instead of jamming your pole into a vault box, it is already jammed into a canal. And rather than trying to jump as high as possible, you have to jump as far as you can. Oh, and if you fail, you don't land on a large, soft cushion, but in a chilly, muddy ditch. That's what canal jumping is all about.

The world center for canal jumping is the Dutch province of Friesland, where the sport is known as *fierljeppen* (*fier* in the local tongue is "far" and *ljeppen* means "leaping"). There have been *fierljeppen* matches for centuries, with written accounts of the sport going back to 1771. The sport was organized into an official championship in 1957. Today, there are six competitive leagues, and the annual National *Fierljepping* Manifestation is the de facto world championships.

A leap of faith

The pole can be anything from 8 – 13 m (26.25 – 42.5 ft) long and is mounted on a flat plate on the canal bottom to prevent it from plunging into the mud. You sprint towards the pole then leap and grab it as high up as you can. Now comes the key maneuver – you must shimmy UP the pole as high as you can, while controlling its direction. The higher up you get, the further across the canal the pole will drop you.

Fierljeppen is like pole vaulting in that it requires a unique mix of agility, strength and flat-out runway speed. There is also quite a technical element – knowing exactly when to be making which move with your body is vital.

The pole vault meets the long jump — over water.

Did you know? The track and field event of pole vaulting actually grew out of canal jumping. Large areas of the Netherlands and the fenlands of England were drained by creating a network of open canals. Farmers needed a way to cross these without getting wet or undertaking a long journey. Rather than build a bridge or run a ferry at every potential crossing point, locals simply kept a supply of jumping poles in their homes. They would travel with these and use them to cross a drainage channel when they came upon one.

221

Flip, flop, fly — and fall over.

The future is here

Just how cool was Marty McFly's hoverboard in *Back to the Future II*? It's been the dream transportation device of movie fans everywhere since 1989. And, after decades of waiting, that dream has finally been made a (slightly wet) reality – thanks to the flyboard.

One of the world's newest extreme watersports, flyboarding was invented in 2011 by former world-champion jet-ski racer, Franky Zapata.

You stand on a board that's connected via a long hose to a jet ski. The watercraft boosts the water up the hose to a pair of boots on the board. These have jet nozzles underneath, through which the water is thrust. This propels you in the opposite direction – up – so that you can swoop, fly and hover up to 15 m (50 ft) above the water.

The overall visual effect is like the Green Goblin in Spiderman but with water whooshing out of his glider. Still, it's terrific fun.

The first world championship was held in 2012 in Qatar and the sport has – quite literally – taken off since then. The newness of the activity means there is plenty of opportunity for you to make your mark in the world championships. You'll need good balance, some gymnastic ability and stamina.

The tricks

You'll also need to learn some of flyboarding's key moves:

Somersaults – Can you flip over without ploughing head-first into the ocean? Can you do it twice in a row?

Spins – Change the angle of one foot so that you rotate around your vertical axis. Just don't spin too fast or you'll wind yourself up your hose like a swingball.

Dives – Lift your feet up, point your head down and plunge into the ocean. The real skill is in flying back up and out again.

Did you know? Inventor Zapata has also created a prototype of a new machine that uses a jet turbine and a 30-m (100-ft) hose, so you can hover high above land as well as water.

Fancy footwork

If you've ever thrown your slipper at a spider and hit the bullseye, clog cobbing could be the world championship sport for you. "Cobbing" is simply the throwing of a traditional wooden-soled, leather-uppered Lancashire clog from between your legs, up and over your head. Furthest throw wins and there are men's, ladies' and children's classes.

Is it a javelin, is it a discus? No, it's super clog.

There are a couple of basic rules:

- You must use two hands to hold your clog.

- You can make as many warm-up swings as you like, but cannot take a run-up.

- The clog must fly up and over your head; no over-the-shoulder or round-the-body throws.

- The clog must land on the "pitch," a rather narrow lane.

How to be a canny cobber

For your best chance at being crowned clog-cobbing champion, there are three key skills that you must learn. First, there's getting the clog to actually go backwards over your head. Novices often let go too soon, sending the clog flying forwards into the crowd or, occasionally straight up in the air and down again on their own heads. Once you can confidently send it flying behind you, the next skill to be mastered is horizontal alignment. The "pitch" is, in reality, a single-track lane. On the left-hand side is a row of trees; on the right is a stone wall, beyond which runs a chattering and rather chilly river. The tree branches will snag your clog and cost you distance. The river will result in disqualification and wet feet. (A ladder is provided so that you can retrieve your errant piece of footwear.) The final ability that marks all clog-cobbing masters is timing. Like a kind of vertical golf swing, all the levers of your arms, legs and torso must be aligned at the perfect time in the cob for you to generate power.

Local knowledge

The event takes place right beside the Roebuck Inn, Waterfoot, on Easter Sunday and is part of a wider celebration that includes tug of war, darts and other traditional events. Much ale tends to be drunk on this occasion, and the advice from a previous champion is to get your clog cobbing done before having too many refreshments. Although your confidence may be raised, your cobbing skills really will not. After about 4 pm, 90 percent of clogs end up in the river. Not that the cobbers seem to mind by that point...

Paint your way to a world title

You may have managed some pretty good butterflies at your last children's party, but, as you can see, you'll need to step up your bodypainting game if you want to be world champ. The first event was held in 1998, and was only attended by a few pioneering bodypaint artists. It proved so popular that it has expanded into a three-day family festival of art, design and fantastically creative imagery.

The highlight of the festival is the World Bodypainting Championships where the *crème de la crème* of artists from over fifty countries create stunning artworks in six categories. There are also Special and Amateur Awards. The championship categories include bodypainting with brush and sponge, airbrush, special effects, make-up and facepainting.

Brush up your skills

Practice, patience and inspiration are the key qualities you will need to make it here. You can choose to adorn either a male or female model, but just make sure that they are comfortable holding a pose for a long time – some complex creations can take eight hours to paint.

"Bodypainting is special because the artwork is alive and can move. While a canvas painting lasts forever, a bodypainting exists only for a few hours. A lot of my inspiration comes from nature. I think the secret of good work is to always have a love for it."

Johannes Stoetter, world bodypainting champion 2013

Did you know? There is a special "World UV Bodypainting Award" category at the festival, where artists use fluorescent colors to make the models glow

You'll need to be wild and wonderfully creative with a willing volunteer.

93 | FOOSBALL

Teams in perfect formation

In student unions, frat houses, hipster bars and cool software companies, there's usually a foosball table. And if you often end the night as righteous ruler of that domain, then it's time for you to realize your miniature soccer potential.

There are several different makes of foosball table (Leonhart, Garlando, Bonzini, Fireball and Roberto Sport) with their own subtle differences in size, shape and configuration, which demand varied playing skills and strategies. If you become a champion in one of these, you could compete for the ultimate foosbal accolade – the Multi-Table World Championships.

This is held in Nantes, France every January and usually draws over 500 players from thirty countries. You can also enter the Multi-Table Championships by earning enough ranking points in smaller events, or by winning your home national championship. In addition, there is an annual world cup competition, competed for by nations, rather than individuals.

The game is played on a table, with eleven little figures on each side mounted on rods. The rods are pushed, pulled and twisted by the players to control a small ball and score goals. There is, of course, NO SPINNING of the rods! That's strictly for amateurs…

Flick and kick your way to victory.

Did you know? You must wear acceptable sporting attire for your matches. Clothes displaying profanity, non-athletic tank tops, jeans of any kind, cargo pants, form-fitting Spandex or Lycra pants and shorts are all prohibited. Flip-flops, sandals and other non-athletic shoes are also a no-no.

Skills to work on

Wrist strength is vital – top players can blast the balls at up to 56 km/h (35 mph) in competition. But raw power isn't everything. Foosball players may be bolted to metal rods a set distance apart, but there are plenty of nifty tricks and shots that you can pull off with practice.

Pull kick shot – Use the side of an attacking player's feet to pull the ball laterally across the pitch, then use a player nearer you to shoot.

Push kick shot – The opposite of the pull kick shot – you push the ball across the pitch from yourself to another player, who shoots.

Snake shot – This is also called a rollover. An attacker traps the ball between feet and table. You then place the handle on your wrist and rapidly pull your arm up. The rod will spin counterclockwise, the player will flip "over the top" and strike the ball into the goal.

Bank shot – Usually taken from defense, this is when you bounce the foosball off the wall at the proper angle to go around the opposition and score a goal.

Aerial shot – A difficult trick shot taken by the defenders. The goalkeeper passes the ball sharply into the heels of the teammate defender in front. When the ball jumps up into the air, the two lift their feet simultaneously to raise the ball. It can then be tipped onto the back of the defender's legs, to be lobbed high up the table into the goal.

94 | CABER TOSSING

WHERE WORLDWIDE | **SINCE** 1980
USEFUL EQUIPMENT TREE TRUNKS, LEGS LIKE TREE TRUNKS

Could this be the year of your tartan triumph?

Remember to eat your porridge

"That larch tree has fallen over," said a Scotsman as he walked through a misty forest one day a long time ago. "I know what, I'm going to pick it up and see how accurately I can throw it." And so the sport of caber tossing was born.

An average caber is around 6 m (19.7 ft) tall and weighs 79 kg (175 lbs). Even standing the thing on one end is hard enough. But you also need to pick it up, not instantly drop it again, then run forwards and throw it high in the air. Not only that, but you have to do so accurately. The ideal caber toss should see it turn end-over-end and land facing directly away from you in the "12 o'clock" position.

Don't worry if you can't quite get your caber to land at 12 o'clock. The caber toss is just one of several traditional events featured in Highland Games gatherings, and you could also try:

- **Weight throw** – All you have to do is throw a lump of iron as far as you can or, in the "over the bar" category, as high as you can. The trouble is that the iron weighs 25.4 kg (56 lb) for men and 12.7 kg (28 lb) for women.
- **Stone put** – Like the modern shot put, but using a very much heavier stone.
- **Scottish hammer throw** – Like the track and field hammer except, again, with a heavier weight, and with a wooden handle rather than a wire one.

Where to do your highland fling

The Cowal Highland Gathering is the largest highland games competition in Scotland, and if you make it in the open classes here, you could be heading for the World Highland Games Championships. This premier event moves between Scottish locations and venues where Scots-descended locals enjoy the traditions, such as Canada, the U.S. and New Zealand.

Did you know? Baron Pierre de Coubertin saw a display of Highland games at the Paris Exhibition of 1889. The events he saw helped inspire him to revive the Olympic Games.

Wacky and messy, in equal measure.

Wait, it has *what* in it?

Many people, when first told what a black pudding actually is, have an instinctive urge to throw it as far away from themselves as they can. For it isn't pudding in the typical sense. Black pudding is actually a mixture of pork fat, beef suet, oatmeal and pork blood. This is formed into a sausage that is then boiled and served with malt vinegar in a paper wrapping. Exactly.

However, it's a popular delicacy in many parts of the UK, and the World Black Pudding Throwing Championships are very much a celebration of the affection in which the dish is held.

It's different from many throwing events in that it isn't about achieving distance, but about accuracy. You have to knock stacks of Yorkshire puddings off a 6-m (20-ft) high plinth with your black puddings. You have three black puddings to throw, and twelve

Yorkshire puddings to knock off. You must throw underarm from the oche, a marked line. Whoever dislodges the most is the winner. (We should point out that a Yorkshire pudding isn't a sweet dish either, but a batter made of eggs, flour and milk that is baked in the oven.)

Legend says that the pudding throwing began in 1455, when warring factions of the houses of Lancaster and York met for battle nearby. For some reason that history does not relate, they decided to settle their grievances by throwing their own favorite local foodstuffs at each other.

No low blows

The first thing to know about cricket fighting is that it isn't a blood sport. Like middle-aged men who should know better, the creatures get a bit agitated, then settle their differences with the insect equivalent of a bit of shouting and shoving. After an initial flurry of leg and antennae waving, one cricket invariably decides it isn't worth the bother and simply wanders off. He is the loser.

It's easier to land a punch when you have six arms.

Seconds away

Like boxers, fighting crickets are assigned to a weight class. Two matched creatures are put into opposite sides of a clear container divided in the middle. Before the match you need to give your cricket's whiskers a rub with a piece of straw. This gets him ready for battle. When both crickets are chirping – equivalent to the "calling-your-mother-names" stage – the divider is lifted and the two crickets begin their match.

Selecting your warrior

The finest fighting crickets are bred in northeastern Shandong Province by keepers who maintain careful records of their pedigrees, just like racehorses. Your fighting cricket will be a male, and you should house him in a clay pot and feed him on high-protein foods such as goat's liver, ground shrimp, red beans and maggots. On the eve of a fight, pop a female cricket into his pot to get his dander up.

Cricket fighting is very much a Chinese obsession, and if you want to be world champ, that's where you and your warring insects will need to prove yourselves. The National Cricket Fighting Championships – the most prestigious competition in the world – are held over two days every year in Beijing. It's a grand affair, and you can field up to thirty-five crickets, each of which must be weighed and labelled with his category beforehand.

Top tip

Academics who have studied the cricket's fighting spirit have found that if the cricket does a bit of flying before a bout it will fight better. Normally when a losing cricket is returned to the ring he will win the second fight only one out of ten times. But if you encourage him to leap around his box a little, he will fight again six times out of ten. However, if you gently tape him to the blade of a rotating ceiling fan and give it a few spins, the cricket will fight ten times out of ten and will almost always win. Maybe boxers should try the same tactic.

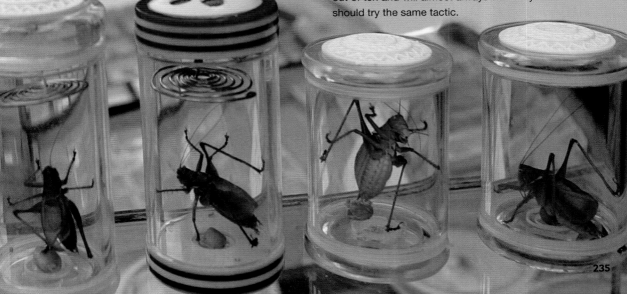

235

Holy good gravy

Wrestling is one of the most ancient and noble of all sports. Since before recorded history, contestants have faced each other in the ring and grappled hand-to-hand, body-to-body to gain dominance and win the crown of champion. But what no ancient civilization had ever thought of was the idea of holding such a chivalrous contest in a pool full of Lancashire gravy.

The organizers used to make the gravy for the contest themselves, but as this was a "bit of a nightmare" they were delighted when famous gravy producers Bisto offered to help. The pool is now filled with 2,000 liters (440 gallons) of Bisto that is past its sell-by date. You have two minutes to wrestle your foe in the tasty brown meat sauce while being scored for your moves and entertainment value.

Slip sliding away

This sport is a unique form of wrestling, in that winning isn't about being a superb athlete and an expert in Greco-Roman techniques. It's more about perfecting a delicate blend of pulling some good moves, putting on a show and having a laugh. Here are the moves you need, with the points they will earn you:

Take Down – 2 points: You have your opponent down in the gravy and are in full control.

Escape – 1 point: Your opponent has you down in the gravy, but you escape the hold.

Reversal – 2 points: Even better than an escape, you get out AND get on top to take control of your opponent.

Fall – 3 points: Holding both of your opponent's shoulders down in the gravy for a 3-second count.

You'll soon get a taste for this sport.

Near Fall – 2 points. Like a fall, but only one shoulder is held in the gravy for a 3-second count.

Fun Factor – up to 20 points. The judges will be generous to contestants who:
• Show the highest fun factor
• Receive the loudest applause
• Raise the biggest laugh
• Have the best costume

Infractions – 1 – 10 penalty points. There are several illegal holds that will be penalized:
• Leaving the paddling pool
• Jumping on opponents
• Pulling clothing
• Locking your hands
• Unnecessary roughness
• Unfair use of props
• Unsportsmanlike conduct

Serious unsportsmanlike conduct will result in your immediate disqualification. As will taking the whole thing too seriously.

A hose-toting crew from the local firehouse provides showering facilities.

"The final was really tough and it is much more difficult than you think. My technique was really just to grab hold of the guy and hope for the best."

Joel Hicks, world champion

Put on your dancing shoes

Almost everyone can move to music (apart from your dad, obviously) and dancing appeals to all ages, cultures and genders. The surge of television shows featuring dancing in recent years has helped its popularity.

Competitive ballroom dancing is built on tradition, panache and elegance. In the 1980s, there were growing numbers of dancers who still respected ballroom's beauties but wanted to move beyond its narrow stylistic confines. In a move that sounds like a terrific idea for a movie, they began dancing in a more creative and athletic way to create "sportdance." One of the most inspired and dramatic categories of sportdance is boogie woogie.

Say, what kind of dancing is this?

Boogie woogie is a smooth-moving type of swing dance powered by a characteristic style of blues piano. But the basic steps are just the start – good boogie woogie dancers will add on an extraordinary suite of athletic moves. With their leaps, spins and throws, boogie woogie dancers seem to get almost as much air as ski jumpers and, what's more, they do it in time to music. In the last twenty years, boogie woogie has powered the glamorous and gorgeous world of competitive sportdance from strength to strength.

World-class moves

Your gateway to world dancing domination is through your country's national championships. If you excel there, then you head off for two days of dancing at the very highest standard at the Boogie Woogie World Championships. There are two main classes: Slow and Fast, as well as special junior and senior sections. The final award ceremony features a free-for-all last dance with hundreds of couples taking to the floor to strut their stuff.

The boogie woogie supporters can be notoriously rowdy, creating an exhilarating atmosphere that is almost anarchic compared with ballroom dancing. Even if you don't win, you'll have an experience you will never ever forget.

And a-one, a-two, a one-two-three-four...

Did you know? If you don't have the oomph to cut it in boogie woogie, you could try tapping your toes to the alternative styles of Rock 'n' Roll, Rock 'n' Roll Acrobatic, Lindy Hop, Bugg and Doublebug.

Do you have the skills to get a slice of the action?

Garlic bread not necessary

Imagine the delight on the face of the famished soul who was served the very first slice of the very first pizza, when it was created in eighteenth-century Italy. *Mamma mia!* The country is still home to the world's finest pizzas, and Naples, the city where this magnificent dish has its humble origins, is the most pizza-obsessed city in Italy. Which makes its annual world pizza championship the most sumptuous feast of pizza adoration on the planet.

A Neapolitan pizza is about as far from the doughy, cheese-sodden lump that you put in your microwave, as champagne is from last week's lukewarm chardonnay. Here, the technical term for a pizza maker is a *pizzaiolo*. The best of them are treated like royalty, and cafes are filled with gossip about who is the best, and who are the rising stars.

The annual pizza championships draw more than 500 competitors from around the world to a specially built village with over fifty wood-fired pizza ovens heating up the already warm Italian air.

If you want to be the premier *pizzaiolo*, your creation will be judged on every possible criterion: kneading, baking, charring, size, thickness, the

puff and bounce of the pizza's *cornichon* (crust), toppings, neatness of your cooking area – and, most importantly, the taste.

Practice makes pizza

Your creation should be deferential to tradition, but also bold and full of inspired passion. Much like the Italians themselves. Oh, and don't even think about making a stuffed-crust – the Neapolitans would never talk to you again. There are several categories in which you can enter:

 classico **with freestyle toppings**

 gluten-free

 pizza-by-the meter

 and the big one – **the Neapolitan**

Even if you don't win, you can still stop by to congratulate your rivals and savor some of the finest bread, tomato and cheese that you will ever taste.

Famous for fibbing

The World's Biggest Liar is an annual championship held at the Bridge Inn, Santon Bridge, England. The event was established in memory of Will Ritson, a local pub landlord in the nineteenth century, who loved to fool travelers with his tall tales. A favorite fib of his was that the local turnips grew so big that farmers harvested them by quarrying into them. The hollowed-out turnips were then used as sheds for their sheep.

Rules of the lie

You have five minutes to tell the tallest – and also the most convincing – tale you can. Props and scripts are not allowed. Politicians and lawyers are banned from entering as they do this for a living and would have an unfair advantage.

You're the favorite for this event.

Lying legends

What makes a championship-winning lie? Your fib should be creative, fantastical, and yet, somehow, rooted in a small truth to make it more believable. Have a look at some of the winning whoppers from recent years to see what you're up against:

George Kemp, a publican from Maryport, took the crown with a tall tale about his wooden car, which "wouldn't start."

Abrie Krueger of South Africa triumphed in 2003 after assuring the judges that he was now the King of the Wasdale Valley. This was the first time that a foreigner had become world champion.

Comedian **Sue Perkins** won the 2006 competition with a story about how the melting ice caps meant that people had to commute to work on camels. She was the first-ever female champion.

John "Johnny Liar" Graham won the competition in 2007 with a story about a Second World War German submarine that had recently invaded Britain to capture digital television decoders. Johnny Liar made it two wins in a row the following year with his yarn about a magical journey he made to Scotland in a wheelie bin that went under the sea.

A tale about a snail race with Prince Charles won the 2011 title for **Glen Boylan**. The heir to the British throne advised Glen to remove his snail's shell to make it more aerodynamic, but he still lost because his opponents cheated by using battery-operated snails.

Mike Naylor won in 2013 with a story about Wassie, the monster that lives in Wastwater, the local lake.

The shortest-ever winning lie was told many years ago by the **Bishop of Carlisle**. He stood up and simply said, "I have never told a lie in my life."

Did you know? Want to save yourself some time? Be honest. A 2009 study found that in 85 percent of cases, people were slower when they lied than when they told the truth.

Flying fingers

Knitting has enjoyed a surge in popularity in recent years, and with good reason. It's creative, practical and devotees are happy to tell of its calming, mindful properties. It's also something that you can do insanely fast, if you practice enough.

The British Hand Knitting Confederation and the Craft Yarn Council of America have agreed on rules for competitive speed knitting. You must use needles that are 4 mm (0.16 in.) around, do the same stocking stitch as other competitors and use the same medium-weight yarn.

A stitch in time

The world championship is fought for in a head-to-head knit-off. That means that if you want to claim the crown you need to beat the current champ, Hazel Tindall from the Shetland Islands. This remote Scottish archipelago is famed for its chunky wool knitwear: before oil brought wealth to the islands, the women knitted as a way to put food on the table. Helen learned to knit before she could read, copying her mother and grandmother. When she saw that the 2002 contest in New York was won by a competitor knitting 180 stitches in three minutes, she knew she could better that. So she came to London for the 2004 championships and destroyed the field with a stunning 255 stitches in three minutes. At the 2008 International World Speed Knitting Championships in Minneapolis, Helen upped this to 262 stitches; her nearest rival knitted only 243.

Top tips for hot knits

If you want to speed up your knitting to championship standard, there are some quirks of the craft that you will need to watch out for:

The jitters – Speed knitting demands fast repetitive movements that can cause your hands to shake. This leads to dropped stitches.

Sweaty palms – Although you're making wool garments, don't wear them. You need to be cool in the competition as sweaty palms and moist fingers can make it tricky to push yarn down your needle. You may want to use talcum powder or hold a cool bottle of water.

Sliding – As you get faster, you may find the wool catches high up on your needle. Use nickel-plated needles and you'll find the yarn slides down more easily.

> "I waved my hands in the air to keep people happy. But I'm not one for showing off. There's plenty of knitters on Shetland faster than me."
>
> Helen Tindall, on becoming world knitting champion

Did you know? According to the Craft Yarn Council of America, 36 percent of women in the U.S. (53 million ladies) know how to knit or crochet. That's a 51 percent increase in the past ten years.

Win a world crown and make a nice hat at the same time.

INDEX

TAKE IT FURTHER

Have you found an event that you know you can master? Then perhaps it's time you signed up for its world championships. Or have you seen something you'd like to try and want to find out more about getting involved? Most of the sports are delighted to welcome newcomers, so we've compiled a list of the official websites of the championship organizers or governing bodies for each event, to help you get in touch. Where there is no such site we have included the most useful online source of information for that activity. We hope you find this helpful on your journey to the podium.

air guitar
www.airguitarworldchampionships.com

alligator wrestling
www.gatorland.com/public/experiences/
rookie-wrestling/index.cfm

baby crawling
www.vileda.com/uk/baby-championship-
competition-terms-conditions

bagpiping
www.theworlds.co.uk/pages/home.aspx

bearding
www.worldbeardchampionships.com

bee wearing
en.wikipedia.org/wiki/bee_bearding

beer mile
www.flotrackbeermile.com

black pudding throwing
calendarcustoms.com/articles/world-black-
pudding-throwing-championships

boardgaming
www.boardgamers.org/#wbc

bodypainting
www.bodypainting-festival.com/en

bog snorkelling
www.green-events.co.uk/events.html?id=57

boogie woogie
www.worlddancesport.org/News/WDSF/2015_
World_Boogie_Woogie-1918

So you want to be a champ? We can help you get started.

caber tossing
www.worldheavyevents.com

cake decorating
www.cakedesignersworldchampionship.com

canal jumping
www.pbholland.com/?&context=alle&lang=en

chainsaw carving
www.uschainsawchamps.com

cheese rolling
www.cheese-rolling.co.uk/the_event.htm

cherry-pit spitting
www.treemendus-fruit.com/album_2_009.htm

chessboxing
worldchessboxing.com

clog cobbing
calendarcustoms.com/articles/rawtenstall-
clog-cobbing-championships

coal carrying
www.gawthorpemaypole.org.uk/?page_id=21

cockroach racing
www.cockroachraces.com.au

combat juggling
www.thewjf.com

conkers
www.worldconkerchampionships.com

cricket fighting
en.wikipedia.org/wiki/cricket_fighting

cycle polo
www.hardcourtbikepolo.com

deer calling
www.wildundhund.de/home/8087-17-
deutsche-meisterschaft-im-hirschrufen

disc golf
www.pdga.com

dog dancing
www.worldcaninefreestyle.org

drone racing
droneworlds.com

dry riverbed racing
henleyontodd.com.au

egg throwing
www.eggthrowing.com/world_championship.php

extreme ironing
www.facebook.com/extremeironingofficial

extreme pogo
xpogo.com

ferret-legging
en.wikipedia.org/wiki/ferret-legging

flyboarding
www.h2romagazine.com/flyboard-world-cup

fly-casting
www.wcflycasting.com/events.html

foosball
www.table-soccer.org

freestyle soccer
freestylefootball.org/albums

goanna pulling
www.goannapulling.com.au/history.html

gravy wrestling
www.worldgravywrestling.com

grits rolling
www.worldgritsfestival.com/index.html

gurning
www.egremontcrabfair.com

handwriting
www.handwritingrepair.info/WHAC/index.html

kaninhop
skhrf.com/englishsit

karaoke
www.karaokeworldchampionships.com

latte art
www.worldlatteart.org

lawnmower racing
www.blmra.co.uk/championships

lifesaving
www.ilsf.org/lifesaving-sport/rescue-series

lumberjacking
en.wikipedia.org/wiki/Lumberjack_World_Championship

lying
www.santonbridgeinn.com/#!the-worlds-bigest-liar/cbic

marbles
www.greyhoundmarbles.com

memory sports
www.worldmemorychampionships.com

mini golf
www.minigolfsport.com

mobile phone throwing
www.mobilephonethrowing.fi

mountain unicycling
unicycling.org/unicon

muggle quidditch
www.usquidditch.org/events/special/world-cup

octopush
www.cmas.org/hockey/hockey-world-championship

ostrich racing
en.wikipedia.org/wiki/ostrich#racing

outhouse racing
www.visitvirginiacitynv.com/events/world-championship-outhouse-races.html

paper plane throwing
www.redbullpaperwings.com

paragliding accuracy
www.pgawc.org

peashooting
www.witcham.org.uk/_sgg/m1m6_1.htm

pig squealing
en.wikipedia.org/wiki/La_Pourcailhade

pillow fighting
www.facebook.com/worldpillowfightchampionships

pizza making
www.pizzanapoletana.org/index_eng.php

pooh sticks
pooh-sticks.com

powersliding
gatebil.no/wpc2014

public speaking
www.toastmasters.org/about/world-championship-of-public-speaking

quizzing
www.worldquizzingchampionships.com

rock, paper, scissors
www.usarps.com

rock stacking
www.llanoearthartfest.org/#!rockstacking/q2p1z

sand sculpting
www.harrisand.org

sheep shearing
www.shearingworld.com/worldchamps/worldchamps.htm

shin kicking
www.olimpickgames.co.uk

shoe repairing
www.ssia.info

shovel racing
www.angelfireresort.com/event/2016-world-championship-shovel-races

sled dog racing
www.furrondy.net/events/world-championship-sled-dog-races

speed knitting
en.wikipedia.org/wiki/knitting

sport stacking
www.thewssa.com

stinging nettle eating
www.bottle-inn.net/#!nettle-eating-bottleinn-nettle/c19qp

stone skimming
www.stoneskimming.com

street luge
www.igsaworldcup.com

sumo suit athletics
www.facebook.com/sumosuitathleticsworldchampionships

swamp soccer
suopotkupallo.fi

taxidermy
www.taxidermy.net/wtc

tent pitching
www.youtube.com/watch?v=kCVi2LGpOwc

tiddlywinks
www.etwa.org

tin bathtub racing
castletown.org.im/tinbaths

toe wrestling
bentleybrookinn.co.uk/toe-wrestling

tree climbing
itcc-isa.com

tree felling
www.wlc-2014.com/node/184

ugliest dog
www.sonoma-marinfair.org/worlds-ugliest-dog

welly wanging
www.upperthong.org.uk/?page_id=404

wife carrying
www.eukonkanto.fi/en

window cleaning
www.iwca.org/page/conventioncontest

wine tasting
sawtc.yolasite.com/the-world-blind-tasting-championships.php

winter swimming
winterswimming.ru/en

wood chopping
www.stihl.co.uk/stihl-timbersportsreg-2015-world-championship-comes-to-poland-in-november.aspx

worm charming
www.wormcharming.com

yo-yo
worlds16.com

SOURCES

air guitar
http://www.airguitarworldchampionships.com

boardgaming
http://www.boardgamers.org/century.htm

bodypainting
http://www.mirror.co.uk/news/world-news/world-bodypainting-champions-stunning-pictures-2029586

bog snorkelling
A competitor on what it takes to be a champion bog snorkeller, at:
https://www.youtube.com/watch?v=8u6SIjaLx-0

cake decorating
http://www.internationalfederationpastry.com/official-rules-the-world-trophy-of-pastry-ice-cream-chocolate-2017/

chainsaw carving
Matthew Crabb, at: https://exmoormagazine.wordpress.com/2011/03/16/exmoor-chainsaw-artist-creates-worlds-largest-wooden-carving-of-the-virgin-mary/

cheese rolling
The Official Guide to the event, at:
http://www.cheese-rolling.co.uk/what_happens.htm

cherry-pit spitting
http://www.treemendus-fruit.com/album_2_010.htm

cockroach racing
Dave Freeman; Neil Teplica; Jennifer Coonce (1999). *100 Things to Do Before You Die: Travel Events You Just Can't Miss.* Rowman & Littlefield. ISBN 978-0-87833-243-4. Retrieved 28 March 2013.

conkers
Ashton Conker Club secretary John Hadman, at: http://www.worldconkerchampionships.com/html/conkers_about.html

Two-times World Conker Champion Charlie Bray, at: http://www.worldconkerchampionships.com/html/conkers_about.html

dry riverbed racing
http://www.bbc.co.uk/news/mobile/uk-england-berkshire-13956481

extreme ironing
https://www.facebook.com/ExtremeIroningOfficial/

ferret-legging
http://www.outsideonline.com/1902036/king-ferret-leggers

gravy wrestling
http://news.bbc.co.uk/1/hi/england/lancashire/8230545.stm

gurning
http://www.egremontcrabfair.com/history.html

Definition taken from the *The English Dialect Dictionary* (EDD), compiled by Joseph Wright, Vol. 2. Oxford University Press, Oxford. 1900.

handwriting
http://www.handwritingrepair.info/WHAC/

kaninhop
http://news.nationalgeographic.com/news/2002/03/0326_0328_bunnyhop_2.html

latte art
Competitor Ian Chagunda on the secret to making great latte art, at: http://www.worldlatteart.org/competitors/

lying
http://www.theguardian.com/travel/blog/2007/nov/21/barefacedliars

memory sports
Simon Reinhard, holder of multiple world memory records, at: http://www.memory-sports.com/blog/interviews/simon-reinhard-interview/

mini golf
Rolf Bergström, course owner for the 2015 championships, at: http://www.minigolfsport.com/video.html

mobile phone throwing
http://www.mobilephonethrowing.fi

mountain unicycling
Kris Holm, *The Essential Guide to Mountain and Trials Unicycling*. Gradient Press, Canada. 2012

paper plane throwing
Veselin Ivanov, Bulgarian engineer and world champion, at: http://www.redbullpaperwings.com/News/The_mighty_Ivanov.html

Model plane instructions at: http://www.dailymail.co.uk/sciencetech/article-2937778/How-fold-record-breaking-paper-plane-Maker-reveals-aerodynamic-secrets-offers-1-000-fly-design-him.html

pizza making
Carol Helstosky, *Pizza: A Global History*. Reaktion Books. 2008

pooh sticks
A.A. Milne, *Winnie-the-Pooh* (1926) Methuen & Co. Ltd. (London)

public speaking
Aditya Maheswaran, Finalist 2015, at: https://www.toastmasters.org/About/World-Championship-of-Public-Speaking

Mohammed Qahtani, World Public Speaking Champion 2015, at: https://www.toastmasters.org/About/World-Championship-of-Public-Speaking

quizzing
http://www.worldquizzingchampionships.com/wqc/questions/

rock stacking
David Allen, professional rock-stacker from Maine, at: http://www.mystatesman.com/news/lifestyles/spires-sprout-along-llano-river-at-rock-stacking-w/nqk2q/

shin kicking
[1] Graham Greenall, event chairman, at: http://www.mirror.co.uk/news/weird-news/most-bizarre-sport-ever-check-5803085

[2] Ben Greenall, event Stickler at: http://www.mirror.co.uk/news/weird-news/most-bizarre-sport-ever-check-5803085

shoe repairing
Alistair King, world champion 2015, at: http://www.mirror.co.uk/news/uk-news/alistair-king-meet-britains-first-6159151

speed knitting
http://www.theguardian.com/travel/2012/nov/02/shetland-craft-trail-shopping

stone skimming
Lydéric Bocquet, *American Journal of Physics*, Vol. 71, No. 2, February 2003.

street luge
https://en.wikipedia.org/wiki/Street_luge

tent pitching
http://www.telegraph.co.uk/travel/725937/Fast-pitch-treasures.html

tin bathtub racing
http://www.bbc.co.uk/news/world-europe-isle-of-man-32796694

toe wrestling
World champion, Alan "Nasty" Nash, at: http://www.theguardian.com/sport/video/2015/jun/15/world-toe-wrestling-championship-video

ugliest dog
Chief judge Brian Sobel, at http://www.sonoma-marinfair.org/worlds-ugliest-dog/

welly wanging
http://www.upperthong.org.uk/?page_id=404

wife carrying
http://www.eukonkanto.fi/en/Rules.html

window cleaning
http://www.ungerglobal.com/clean/en/these-are-the-recently-crowned-world-champions-of-speed-cleaning/

wine tasting
http://www.expatica.com/es/news/Spain-wins-world-wine-tasting-contest-debutants-US-come-last_511787.html

yo-yo
http://wtkr.com/2015/09/24/utah-college-student-wins-world-yo-yo-championship/

PICTURE CREDITS

Page 12: Action Press / REX Shutterstock
Page 14–15: © ChinaFotoPress / Getty
Pages 16–17: © epa european pressphoto agency b.v. / Alamy
Page 18: © epa european pressphoto agency b.v. / Alamy
Page 19: © Pete Titmuss / Alamy
Pages 20–21: © LEON NEAL / Getty
Pages 22–23: © epa european pressphoto agency b.v. / Alamy
Pages 24–25: © Felix Stensson / Alamy
Page 25: © Peter Etchells / Alamy
Page 26: © Jeff J Mitchell / Getty
Page 27: © Ross Gilmore / Alamy
Page 28: (top) © Galushko Sergey / Shutterstock
Page 28: (bottom) © Ross Gilmore / Alamy
Page 29: (top) © Jm Teychenne / Getty
Page 29: © otorolka / Shutterstock
Page 30: (top right) © Chris Parsons / Getty
Page 30: (bottom left) © Alexander Mazurkevich / Shutterstock
Page 31: © WENN Ltd / Alamy
Page 33: © Nickolay Vinokurov / Shutterstock
Page 34: © Elena Solovova / Alamy
Page 35: © Daniel Berehulak / Getty
Page 36: (left) © NFU Countryside / Farm Africa
Page 36: (right) © Jana Guothova / Shutterstock
Page 37: © Nick Turner / Alamy
Pages 38–39: © Rob Watkins / Alamy
Pages 40–41: © BeerFit
Page 42: (top) © Matt Child / Alamy
Page 43: © dpa picture alliance / Alamy
Page 44: (top) © M L Pearson / Alamy
Page 44: (bottom left) © simonox / Shutterstock
Page 44: (bottom right) © VECTOR ICONS / Shutterstock
Page 45: © Virginia City Tourism Commission
Pages 46–47: © Phil YEomans / REX Shutterstock
Page 48: © Tony Worpole / Alamy

Page 49: © RomboStudio / Shutterstock
Page 50: © Eric Isselee / Shutterstock
Pages 50–51: © Stanley Chou / Getty
Pages 52–53: © REX Shutterstock
Page 54: © age fotostock / Alamy
Pages 56–57: © villorejo / Alamy
Pages 58–59: © Scott Barbour / Getty
Pages 60–61: © Richard Happer
Page 62: © Richard Happer
Page 63: © Marion Kaplan / Alamy
Pages 64–65: © Richard Ellis / Alamy
Pages 66–67: © Vova Pomortzeff / Alamy
Pages 68–69: © Dudarev Mikhail / Shutterstock
Pages 70–71: © Jeff Morgan 05 / Alamy
Pages 72–73: © Wayne Rowlands
Pages 74–75: © Roger Cracknell 01 / Alamy
Page 76: © Nick Turner / Alamy
Page 77: © Portland Press Herald / Getty
Pages 78–79: © PANIGALE / Shutterstock
Pages 80–81: © Anatoli Styf / Shutterstock
Pages 82–83: © HEIKKI SAUKKOMAA / Getty
Pages 84–85: © Lucas Oleniuk / Getty
Page 87: © incamerastock / Alamy
Pages 88–89: © Barry Bland / Alamy
Pages 90–91: © Nejron Photo / Shutterstock
Pages 92–93: © Richard Happer
Pages 94–95: © Richard Happer
Pages 96–97: © epa european pressphoto agency b.v. / Alamy
Pages 98–99: © Annette Shaff / Shutterstock
Pages 100–101: © Surf Life Saving Australia
Pages 102–103: © Ton Koene/VWPics / Alamy
Pages 104–105: © Outdoor-Archiv / Alamy
Pages 106–107: © Deutscher Minigolfsport Verband
Pages 108–109: © Wooli Sports Club Inc
Pages 110–111: © John Lawson, Belhaven / Getty
Pages 112–113: © Christian Kober / Getty
Pages 114–115: © South West News Service / REX Shutterstock
Pages 116–117: © Michael Sewell / Getty
Pages 118–119: © Carolyn Jenkins / Alamy
Pages 120–121: © FABRICE COFFRINI / Getty
Pages 122–123: © Jeff Lutkus
Pages 124–125: © Photofusion / REX Shutterstock
Pages 126–127: © John A. Beatty / Getty